LANGUAGE BUILDER

In Sync 2

Rod Fricker
Ingrid Freebairn
Jonathan Bygrave
Judy Copage

Welcome to the **Language Builder!**

This **Language Builder** will give you more practice in the grammar, vocabulary, functions, and skills that are in your Student Book. The Language Builder is divided into two parts: a Workbook and a Grammar Bank.

Workbook

The first part of the Language Builder is the **Workbook**. This contains practice exercises for the grammar, vocabulary, functions, and skills in your Student Book. Most of the exercises in the Workbook lessons are at two levels of difficulty: easier (★) and more difficult (★★). There are also *Consolidation* exercises, which provide practice of several language points. In addition, there is an *Extra challenge!* exercise (★★★) in each unit, which gives you the opportunity to do a more challenging activity.

Grammar Bank

The second part of the Language Builder is the **Grammar Bank**. This contains *Grammar Summary* pages with examples and notes to help you remember grammar rules. These are followed by *Grammar Practice* exercises. You can do these exercises as a follow-up to the exercises in the Workbook, or you can use them later to help you review.

We hope that this Language Builder will help you in your English studies.

Have fun and stay *In Sync*!

Contents

Contents

He goes to my school.

Phrases

1 ★ Complete the conversations with the correct phrases from the box.

> • How are you • I have to go • I'm fine
> • Nice to meet you • See you later • this is

1 A: Hello, Mark.
  How are you ?
  B: OK, thanks. And you?

2 A: Hi, Jackie. Are you OK?
  B: Yes. _____ ,
  thanks.

3 A: Natalie, _____
  my friend Carlos.
  B: Hi, Carlos. _____
  _____ .

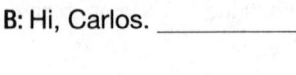

4 A: Bye, Megan.
  B: Bye, Fiona. _____
  _____ .

5 A: Look! There's my dad.
  _____ .
  B: OK, Sara. See you later.

Vocabulary: Family

2 ★ Complete the chart with the correct family words.

Male 👤	Female 👤	Male and female 👤👤
father	1 _mother_	2
3	grandmother	4
brother	5	
6	aunt	
7	niece	
husband	8	
son	9	10
		cousins

Vocabulary: Countries and nationalities

3 ★ Complete the country and nationality words.

> I have lots of friends on the Internet. Most of my friends are 1 Ame_rican_ or 2 Can_____ ,
> but I have friends from other countries, too. From Asia, there's Hohki from 3 Ja_____
> and Xia from 4 Ch_____ . I have some friends from South America, too. Luisa and
> Hector are 5 Col_____ , Maria is 6 Arg_____ , and Amelia and Juan are 7 Br_____ . And
> I have three friends from 8 Mex_____ : Jorge, Diego, and Alicia. Oh, and I have two new
> friends from Europe: Igor is 9 Ru_____ and 10 Emily is Br_____ . I love the Internet!

Grammar: Simple present

4 ★ Complete the conversation with the correct form of the verbs in parentheses.

Tim: Two students want to be student-council president. Jason's in my class. He **1** *likes* (like) sports and music. He **2** _____ (play) for the school football team and he **3** _____ (sing) in a band. He **4** _____ (speak) excellent Spanish. He **5** _____ (not wear) very nice clothes, and his hair is long.

Beth: **6** _____ he _____ (work) hard?

Tim: Not always, but he's a good student. The second student is Carrie. Carrie's in 11th grade, too. She **7** _____ (work) very hard, and she always **8** _____ (get) good grades. She **9** _____ (not play) any sports, and she **10** _____ (not speak) Spanish. She always **11** _____ (wear) very nice clothes, and all the students like her.

Beth: What **12** _____ she _____ (do) in her free time?

Tim: She studies and reads a lot. So, what do you think?

Consolidation

5 Complete the paragraph with the words from the box.

> • doesn't • don't • go • goes • ~~is~~ • likes • live
> • Mexican • Mexico • speaks • work • works

I have three friends at school. Teresa **1** *is* from Mexico City in **2** _____ . Her father is **3** _____ , but her mother is American. Now her parents **4** _____ in the U.S. and Teresa **5** _____ to my school. She **6** _____ Spanish and English. She **7** _____ the U.S., but she wants to go back to Mexico. Her father **8** _____ in a factory. Her mother **9** _____ work. Mick and Jason are Canadian. They're from Vancouver. Their parents **10** _____ in a hospital here. They **11** _____ like the U.S. very much, but I'm very happy that they **12** _____ to my school.

Extra challenge!

6 ★★★ Look at the profile of Lionel Messi. Write questions and answers.

Name:	Lionel Messi
Nationality:	Argentinian
From:	Rosario, Argentina
Team:	Barcelona
Languages:	Spanish
Girlfriend:	Antonella Roccuzzo

1 What / nationality / be / Lionel Messi?

What nationality is Lionel Messi?

He's Argentinian.

2 Where / be / he / from?

_____

_____

3 Which team / he / play for?

_____

_____

4 What languages / he / speak?

_____

_____

5 What / be / his girlfriend's name?

_____

_____

Vocabulary: Daily routines

1 ★ Look at the pictures. Match the verbs (1–10) to the phrases (a–j) to make daily routines.

1 get _b_	a) breakfast
2 have __	b) home from school
3 do __	c) to bed
4 leave __	d) up
5 watch __	e) in bed
6 go __	f) your teeth
7 wake __	g) school
8 brush __	h) to music
9 read __	i) TV
10 listen __	j) your homework

Grammar: Adverbs and expressions of frequency

2 ★ Circle the correct words to complete the sentences.

1 I play video games (every) / once day.

2 We have lunch once a / two times day.

3 Linda goes to Mexico twice / twice a year.

4 Peter and Mark exercise twice / three times a week.

3 ★ Complete the paragraph with the adverbs of frequency from the box.

> • always • always • hardly ever • never
> • often • sometimes • usually • usually

When I get up, I **1** _always_ take a shower (every day). I **2** _____ have toast for breakfast (nine times out of ten).

I **3** _____ drink coffee (I hate it).

I **4** _____ drink milk (four or five times a week), but I **5** _____ drink tea (two or three times a week).

After school, I **6** _____ go home (almost every day). I **7** _____ go out on school days (about once a year) because our teacher **8** _____ gives us lots of homework (every day).

4 ★★ Answer the questions using the information in parentheses.

Our habits
How often . . .

1 do you brush your teeth? (3x day)

I brush my teeth three times a day.

2 does your class have a test? (1x week)

_____

3 do you have breakfast? (2x week)

_____

4 does your mother watch TV? (hardly ever)

_____

5 do you play sports during breaks? (usually)

_____

6 are you late for school? (hardly ever)

_____

Vocabulary: The time

5 ★ Complete the second sentence so that it gives the same time as the first.

1 It's two ten. It's _ten past_ two.

2 It's seven thirty. It's _____ seven.

3 It's eight thirty-five. It's _____ nine.

4 It's a quarter to ten. It's _____ -five.

5 It's one fifteen. It's _____ one.

6 It's two twenty. It's _____ two.

7 It's one fifty-five. It's _____ two.

8 It's three fifty. It's _____ four.

9 It's ten A.M. It's _____ in the morning.

10 It's midnight. It's _____ at night.

Consolidation

6 Look at the pictures. Complete the sentences using the cues.

1 always / never

When I go to school, I _always get up at six thirty_ .

When I'm on vacation, I _never get up at six thirty_ .

2 2x a week / 5–6x a week

When I go to school, _____

_____ .

When I'm on vacation, _____

_____ .

3 rarely / every day

When I go to school, _____

_____ .

When I'm on vacation, _____

_____ .

4 2x a week / 2x a month

When I go to school, _____

_____ .

When I'm on vacation, _____

_____ .

5 1x a month / often

When I go to school, _____

_____ .

When I'm on vacation, _____

_____ .

6 always / never

When I go to school, _____

_____ .

When I'm on vacation, _____

_____ .

1c We're having a barbecue.

Vocabulary: Leisure activities

1 ★ **Rearrange the letters to make activities.**

1 atwhc a VDD *watch a DVD*
2 ypal eht utrgia _____
3 frsu het ent _____
4 ahct ennoil _____
5 ylap eovdi sameg _____
   _____
6 ahev a ueeabbrc _____
7 agnh tuo itwh drnfsie _____
   _____
8 og nhpisogp _____
9 tadasekorb _____
10 og ogngjig _____

2 ★★ **Complete the paragraph with one or two words from the box in each blank.**

> • go • go • go • have • listen • play
> • to • to • ~~watch~~

What do I do in my free time?

I don't often **1** *watch* TV. I usually **2** _____ music on my cell phone. Sometimes, I **3** _____ the guitar at the youth club. In the summer, I **4** _____ the beach with my friends. We **5** _____ swimming every day. My friends sometimes **6** _____ parties at their houses. I don't. My parents always say "No!" There's one thing I never do. I never **7** _____ dancing. I hate it.

Grammar: Present continuous

3 ★ **What are the people doing? Complete the sentences using the verbs in parentheses.**

1 I'*m playing basketball* . (play)

2 They _____ the net. (surf)

3 Sara _____ with her friends online. (chat)

4 I _____ . (jog)

5 My friends and I _____ . (skateboard)

6 My parents _____ a barbecue. (have)

4 ★★ Write the correct form of the verbs.

From:	Tessa
☰▾ **To:**	Jackie

Hi, Jackie!

What **1** <u>_are_</u> you <u>_doing_</u> (do) right now? **2** _____

you _____ (surf) the net? We're all having a

lazy day here. Mom and Dad **3** _____ (have)

a barbecue with some friends. Tommy

4 _____ (skateboard). My cousins

5 _____ (play) basketball—well, not Louise.

She **6** _____ (not play) basketball.

She **7** _____ (sit) on the grass with her

friends Katie and Lana. They **8** _____

(not do) anything special. What **9** _____

I _____ (do) in the house? I **10** _____

(make) tea and coffee for everyone. I have to go!

Bye!

Use your English: Make and respond to requests

5 ★ Complete each conversation with a word from the box.

• <s>Can</s> • can't • certainly • Could • course • Never • please • sorry • Thank

1 A: **1** <u>_Can_</u> you help me, **2** _____ ?

   B: Yes, of **3** _____ .

   A: **4** _____ you.

2 A: **5** _____ you buy me some chocolate at

      the store, please?

   B: Yes, **6** _____ .

3 A: Could you loan me ten dollars, please?

   B: I'm **7** _____ , I can't. I don't have any money.

   A: OK. **8** _____ mind.

4 A: Can you help me with my computer, please?

   B: I'm sorry, I **9** _____ . I don't know

      anything about computers.

Consolidation

6 Look at the pictures. Write questions and answers.

1 What<u>_'s she doing_</u> ?

   She<u>_'s listening to music_</u> .

2 What _____ ?

   It _____ .

3 What _____ ?

   He _____ .

4 What _____ ?

   They _____ .

Across cultures
We all love football.

Before you read

1 Before you read, check the meaning of these words.

> **New words**
> • to download • everyone • expensive • movie • park (*n*)
> • party • to rent

Read

2 ★ Match the headings (1–3) to the correct sections of the letter (A–C).

1 Sports   2 Movies   3 Music

Dear Luke,
Thanks for your postcard about life in the U.K. Here are some facts about me and my friends here in the U.S.

A _____
Most of my friends listen to rock, rap, and hip-hop. We hate pop music! We all have CD players, but 75% of my friends usually download music from the net. We sometimes make CDs for each other. I usually get two or three CDs a week from my friends. My friends like Jay-Z, the Black Eyed Peas, and Beyoncé. In my class, everyone likes the Jonas Brothers. They're from New Jersey. My friend Ben loves Miley Cyrus. She sings pop songs (but good pop songs!).

B _____
We all love football. We play it, we watch it, we talk about it. Only about 5% of my friends go to games because the tickets are expensive! But everyone watches games on TV, especially the Super Bowl. There's a big park near our school, and we often play sports there after school—basketball, baseball, and football, of course! We sometimes go swimming at the local swimming pool on the weekends.

C _____
Most people go to the movies once a week. My friends like Matt Damon (the Bourne films), Ben Stiller, Robert Pattinson, Kristen Stewart, and Taylor Lautner. About 50% of the class like teen movies. All my friends rent DVDs once a month or more, and we often have movie parties on Saturday nights.

See you soon here in the U.S.!
Matt

Miley Cyrus

Kristen Stewart

3 ★★ **Read the text again. Answer the questions.**

1 Where does Luke live? *In England*

2 What kinds of music do Matt's friends like?

_____

3 Who likes Miley Cyrus? _____

4 What is Matt's favorite sport? _____

5 Why don't Matt and his friends go to many games? _____

6 How often do people go to the movies?

_____

7 What do Matt and his friends do on Saturday nights? _____

Listen

4 ★ 🎧 ② **Luke is now in the U.S. with Matt. He asks Matt some questions about his letter. Listen and circle the correct topic for each question he asks.**

1 a) The Jonas Brothers   (b) Miley Cyrus

2 a) American soccer   b) American football

3 a) The Super Bowl   b) The World Cup

4 a) teen movies   b) movie parties

5 a) movie party   b) dance party

5 ★★ 🎧 ② **Listen again and complete the sentences.**

1 Miley Cyrus is a singer and an *actress* .

2 Miley writes her own _____ .

3 People in England usually don't play_____ .

4 The Super Bowl is an important _____ .

5 Luke wants to have a _____ .

6 Luke's favorite actors are _____ and _____ .

Write

> **Writing tip: Conjunctions: *and, or, but, so, because***
>
> **Remember!** We can join two ideas in one sentence by using conjunctions such as *and, or, but, so,* and *because*.
> *On Monday I go to school **and** my friend's house.*
> *On Saturday we go shopping **or** to the movies.*
> *I sometimes watch TV, **but** I often do other things.*
> *I'm not usually tired, **so** I often go to bed late.*
> *I have a snack after school **because** I'm hungry.*

6 ★ **Match the beginnings (1–5, 6–10) with the correct endings (a–e, f–j).**

1 I want to see a funny movie and *d*

2 I want to see a movie, but ___

3 I want to see a movie or ___

4 I want to see a movie, so ___

5 I want to see a movie because ___

6 They're listening to music and *j*

7 They're listening to music, but ___

8 They're listening to music or ___

9 They're listening to music, so ___

10 They're listening to music because ___

a) I don't know which one.

b) I love movies.

c) let's see what's on at the movies.

d) an action movie. I want to see two movies!

e) a TV show.

f) I don't think it's rock music.

g) watching TV.

h) Jack has a new CD.

i) they can't hear me.

j) playing video games at the same time.

7 ★★ **Write answers to the questions using words from the box and the words in parentheses.**

> • a lot / time for other things   • *Avatar* / exciting
> • basketball / football   • ~~bedroom / kitchen~~
> • have / spend a lot of time surfing the net

1 Where do you usually read? (or)
I usually read in my bedroom or in the kitchen .

2 What sports do you play at school? (and)
We _____ .

3 What's your favorite movie? (because)
My _____

_____ .

4 Do you get a lot of homework? (but)
I _____

_____ .

5 Do you have a computer? (so)
I _____

_____ .

People are watching me.

Grammar: Simple present and present continuous

1 ★ Complete the paragraph with the correct form of the verbs. Then write the names of the people in the picture (A–E).

We **1** _'re having_ (have) a great time. We usually

2 _____ (have) a test on Friday afternoons, but

today I **3** _____ (play) soccer with Jason. He

4 _____ (play) soccer every day. He's very good.

Lisa usually **5** _____ (study) in the afternoons, but

today she **6** _____ (not do) any school work. She

7 _____ (read) a book. Chris **8** _____

(swim). He **9** _____ (go) swimming every day,

but he **10** _____ (not usually go) swimming in

a river! We **11** _____ (not usually eat) outside,

but today we **12** _____ (have) a barbecue.

Rob's cooking. I love barbecues.

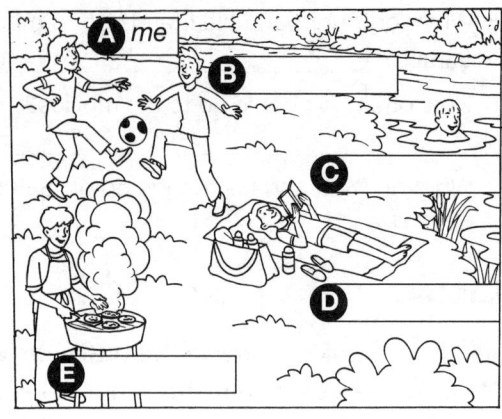

2 ★★ Write questions and answers.

1 A: What / you / do / right now?

What are you doing right now?

B: cook   _I'm cooking._

2 A: Where / Barbara / go / now?

_____

B: to the beach

_____

3 A: What time / your father / usually / get up?

_____

B: usually / at seven o'clock

_____

4 A: Who / your brother / talk / to right now?

_____

B: his friend

_____

5 A: How often / your parents / watch TV?

_____

B: every day

_____

3 ★★ Complete the conversation with the correct form of the verbs *teach*, *speak,* or *have*.

Sam: Hello, Mr. Wright. What are you doing here? You **1** _don't teach_ us on Mondays.

Mr. Wright: Hello, Sam. I **2** _____ this class today.

Sam: Where's Ms. Beauchamp?

Mr. Wright: She **3** _____ today. She's out sick. So I'm here.

Sam: **4** _____ you _____ French?

Mr. Wright: Yes, I **5** _____ , but I **6** _____ French today. You **7** _____ a test today.

Sam: A test? We **8** _____ tests in this class. Ms. Beauchamp doesn't like tests.

Mr. Wright: Really? That's strange. I have a note from Ms. Beauchamp here. It says: "The students in class 3B always **9** _____ a test on Monday afternoons. Please give them test five on page 67. Be careful. Sam usually **10** _____ the answers in his backpack."

Sam: Oh!

Vocabulary: Jobs

4 ★ Circle the correct words.

1 I don't go out to work. I'm a . . .

   (a) stay-at-home mom.) b) plumber.   c) beautician.

2 I type letters for Dr. Martin. I'm his . . .

   a) builder. b) administrative assistant. c) cashier.

3 I serve people food in a restaurant. I'm a . . .

   a) sales clerk.   b) chef.   c) waitress.

4 I write stories for a newspaper. I'm a(n) . . .

   a) dentist.   b) engineer.   c) journalist.

5 I look after sick animals. I'm a . . .

   a) doctor.   b) teacher.   c) vet.

6 I work in a bank. I'm a . . .

   a) cashier.   b) detective.   c) teacher.

7 I fix problems with cars. I'm a(n) . . .

   a) electrician.   b) mechanic.   c) plumber.

5 ★★ Look at the pictures and complete the sentences with the correct jobs.

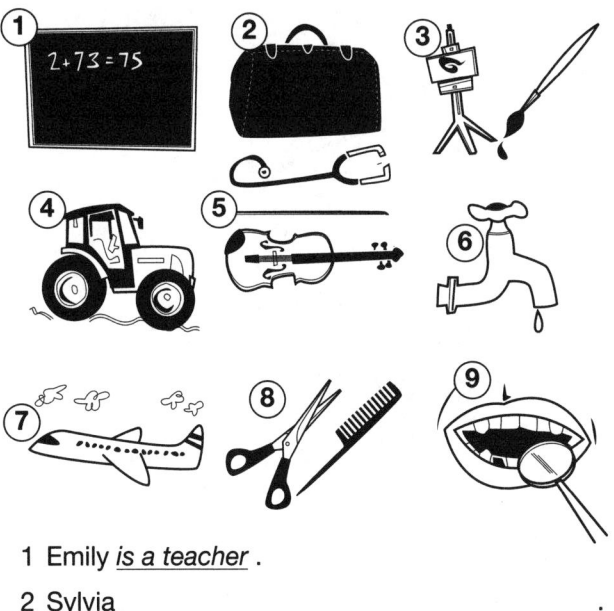

1 Emily *is a teacher* .

2 Sylvia _____ .

3 Martin _____ .

4 Fred _____ .

5 Julia _____ .

6 Tomás _____ .

7 Simon _____ .

8 Luz _____ .

9 Victoria _____ .

Consolidation

6 Write the questions and answers. Then write the person's job in the box.

1 A: you / work in an office? | dentist |

   B: ✗

   A: What / you / do / right now?

   B: I / look / at someone's teeth!

   A: *Do you work in an office?*

   B: *No, I don't.*

   A: *What are you doing right now?*

   B: *I'm looking at someone's teeth!*

2 A: What / Anita / do / now? | _____ |

   B: She / cook / dinner

   A: Where / she / work every day?

   B: She work / in a restaurant, but she / not cook

   A: _____

   B: _____

   A: _____

   B: _____

3 A: you always / wear a white coat? | _____ |

   B: ✓

   A: What / you / do / now?

   B: I / look / at this dog's leg

   A: _____

   B: _____

   A: _____

   B: _____

4 A: Charles work / outside? | _____ |

   B: ✓

   A: What / he / do / now?

   B: He / drive / a tractor

   A: _____

   B: _____

   A: _____

   B: _____

Vocabulary: Money

1 ★ Write the prices in words.

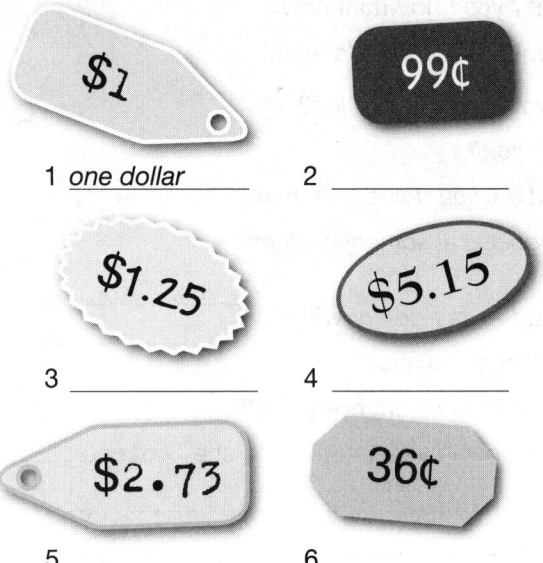

1 _one dollar_   2 _____

3 _____   4 _____

5 _____   6 _____

Vocabulary: Everyday objects

2 ★ Look at the pictures and complete the crossword puzzle.

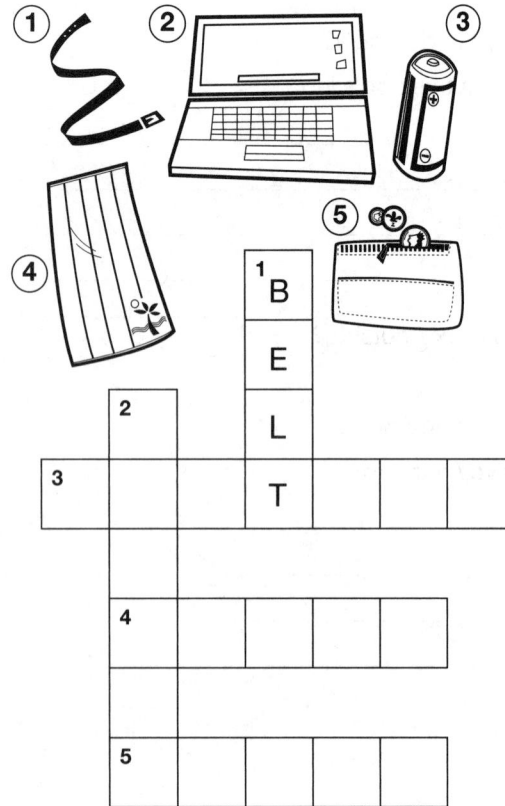

3 ★★ Complete the sentences with the words from the box.

> • bracelets • earring • goggles • necklace • radio
> • sunglasses • wallet

1 My brother always wears an _earring_ in one ear.

2 Do you wear _____ when you're swimming?

3 She's wearing a silver _____ around her neck.

4 Where are my _____ ? It's very sunny today.

5 I have all my money and cards here in my _____ .

6 She has three _____ on her right arm!

7 Do you listen to the _____ in the morning?

Grammar: _whose . . . ?_; Possessive _'s_ and _s'_

4 ★ Follow the lines from the objects to the people and write the correct possessive form.

1 _Pete's_____ book   5 _____ keys

2 _____ pens   6 _____ goggles

3 _____ diary   7 _____ watches

4 _____ T-shirt

12

Grammar: Possessive pronouns

5 ★★ **Complete the conversations about the people in Exercise 4. Use *whose* and possessive pronouns.**

1 Jackie: *Whose book is this?*

  Pete: *It's mine.*

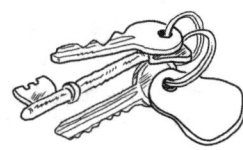

2 Pete: *Whose keys are these?*

  Cousins: *They're hers.*

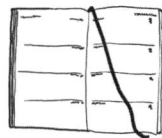

3 Pete: _____

  Jackie: _____

4 Jackie: _____

  Cousins: _____

5 Pete: _____

  Jackie: _____

6 Cousins: _____

  Pete: _____

7 Pete: _____

  Cousins: _____

Use your English: Shop at a store

6 ★ **Complete the conversation.**

1 Sales clerk: Can / help? *Can I help you?*

2 Customer: Excuse / have / radios?

_____

_____

3 Sales clerk: Sorry / not / have / radios.

  have / CD player

_____

_____

4 Customer: much / it? _____

5 Sales clerk: It / $120 _____

6 Customer: No / thanks _____

Consolidation

7 **Complete the second conversation so that it has the same meaning as the first one. Write the names of the objects and the price in words.**

1 **A:** Who owns this ⬚ ?

  B: It belongs to David.

  A: *Whose* is this *laptop* ?

  B: It's *David's* .

2 **A:** Who do these ⬚ belong to?

  B: They belong to us.

  A: _____ _____ are these?

  B: They're _____ .

3 **A:** What's the price of this ⬚ ?

  B: $9.50.

  A: How _____ ?

  B: It's _____ .

4 **A:** Who do these ⬚ belong to?

  B: My parents.

  A: Whose _____ are these?

  B: They're _____ .

Vocabulary: Food and drink

1 ★ Circle the word that doesn't belong.

1 apples   bananas   (eggs)   grapes

2 carrots   onions   potatoes   oranges

3 soda   coffee   ice cream   milk

4 yogurt   vinegar   milk   cheese

5 beans   hot dogs   beef   chicken

6 pears   melon   peaches   lettuce

7 peas   nuts   beans   carrots

2 ★★ Complete the sentences with the correct food words.

1 A: What's for dinner?

B:  _Roast beef_, _____,

   and  _____.

2 I always have a healthy breakfast. I have

 _____,  _____,

and _____.

3 A: I never eat meat.

   B: What do you eat?

   A: _____,  _____,

      or  _____.

4 I love summer fruits. My favorite fruits are

 _____,  _____,

and _____.

Grammar: Count and noncount nouns with *some*, *any*, and *no*

3 ★ Look at the picture and write sentences about the foods below using *there is* or *there are*.

1 (CHEESE) _There's some cheese._

2 (CARROTS) _There aren't any carrots._

3 (EGGS) _____

4 (SUGAR) _____

5 (HONEY) _____

6 (RICE) _____

7 (APPLES) _____

8 (BUTTER) _____

9 (OLIVE OIL) _____

4 ★★ Write questions and answers about the store in Exercise 3. Follow the examples. Use the correct form of *there is* or *there are* and *some*, *any*, or *no*.

1 (bananas?)

A: *Are there any bananas?*

B: *Yes, there are. There are some bananas.*

2 (cookies)

A: *Are there any cookies?*

B: *No, there aren't. There are no cookies.*

3 (pasta)

A: _____

B: _____

4 (salt)

A: _____

B: _____

5 (pears)

A: _____

B: _____

6 (peas)

A: _____

B: _____

7 (bottled water)

A: _____

B: _____

8 (beef)

A: _____

B: _____

Consolidation

5 Complete the conversation.

Gail: Look, there's the new fast-food restaurant. Come on, let's try it.

Penny: OK. Mm, it looks good.

Server: Hello, can I help you?

Gail: Yes. **1** (have / burgers?) *Do you have any burgers?*

Server: Of course.

Gail: Great. A burger and french fries, please.

Server: Oh, sorry. **2** (there / no / french fries) _____

Gail: No french fries!

Server: **3** (there / no / potatoes) _____ _____ today, but **4** (there / rice) _____

Gail: With burgers? No, thank you.

Penny: I don't want a burger. **5** (there / chicken?) _____

Server: **6** (No / not / chicken) _____

Penny: What do you have?

Server: Just burgers.

Penny: **7** (there / soda?) _____

Server: **8** (no) _____ **9** (There / not / drinks) _____

Gail: Come on. Let's go to the old fast-food restaurant. This one's terrible.

Extra challenge!

6 ★★★ Write a conversation in your notebook. Begin like this:

A: *Are there any eggs?*

> **A** You want to make some ice cream. Ask your friend about: eggs, milk, strawberries, sugar.

> **B** You look in the refrigerator. You can see eggs, sugar, and butter, but not milk or strawberries.

INTEGRATED CONSOLIDATION SKILLS

Locavores

Before you read

1 Before you read, check the meaning of these words.

> **New words**
> • average • climate • distance • field • foreign • to freeze • fuel • global warming • same

Can locavores survive in the U.K.?

The word *locavore* comes from San Francisco in California. Locavores try to eat local food. That isn't difficult in this part of the U.S., because there's a lot of farmland. Fruit and vegetables grow in the fields, animals live happily in the Californian climate, and the sea has lots of fish. The locavores freeze food in the summer so that they always have food during the winter. They want to help the fight against global warming. "Most food comes from many different countries. Some is local, but some comes from thousands of miles away. The average distance each item of food travels is 1,500 miles! That's a lot of fuel," says one of the group.

Now some people from the U.K. want to try this idea. "Meat and dairy products are no problem," says Reg Smythe from Birmingham. "The only thing we can't have is foreign fruit like bananas, melons, or grapes. And we can only eat strawberries in June when they grow in the U.K., but that's all right. There's something exciting when you eat the first strawberry of the year. Supermarkets sell South African strawberries in December. It's not the same!"

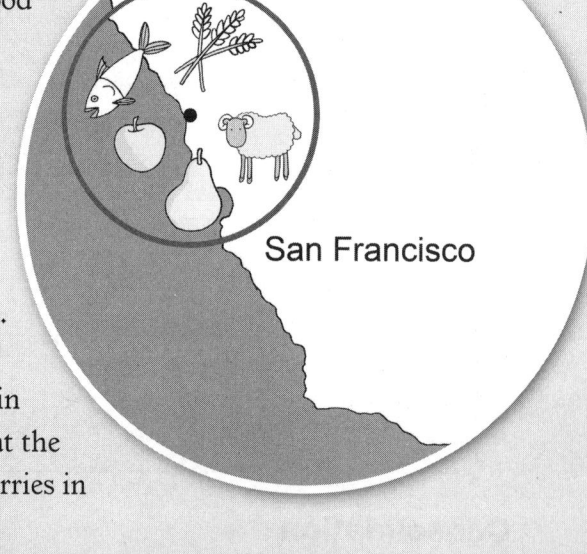

San Francisco

herbivore

carnivore

locavores

Read

> **Learning strategy: Predict from photos, titles, and maps**
> **Remember!** Before you read, look at any photos, titles, and maps. Think about the topic and try to predict what the text is about. This will help you to understand it.

2 ★ Look at the photos, title, and map in Exercise 1. Circle the answers you think are correct.

1 Herbivores . . .
   a) eat meat.   (b) don't eat meat.
2 Carnivores . . .
   a) eat meat.   b) don't eat meat.
3 Locavores eat . . .
   a) food from all over the world.
   b) only food grown locally.
4 The locavore movement comes from . . .
   a) Birmingham.   b) San Francisco.
5 The article is about . . .
   a) the U.S. and U.K.
   b) the U.S. only.

3 ★ Read the article and check your answers to Exercise 2.

4 ★★ Read the article again and circle the correct answers.

1 It's _____ to be a locavore in San Francisco.
   (a) easy   b) difficult   c) impossible
2 In the winter, locavores eat _____ .
   a) frozen food from the supermarket
   b) food from other countries
   c) food that they freeze in the summer
3 Most food comes from _____ .
   a) 1,500 miles away
   b) the local area
   c) all over the world
4 British locavores have problems with
   _____ .
   a) fruit   b) dairy products   c) meat

5 Reg Smythe _____ .
   a) doesn't like strawberries
   b) is excited by strawberries from South Africa
   c) thinks it's best to wait for strawberries from the U.K.

Listen

5 ★ 🎧 3 Listen to five people talking about where they shop and match each to the correct sentence (a–e).

Speaker 1 ___e___   a) I do my shopping by computer.
Speaker 2 _____   b) I go to the farmers' market.
Speaker 3 _____   c) We don't need stores.
Speaker 4 _____   d) The people in the stores know me.
Speaker 5 _____   e) I go with my mom and dad.

Write

6 ★ Look at the map. On a piece of paper, write a paragraph about where the food comes from. Imagine you are in London.

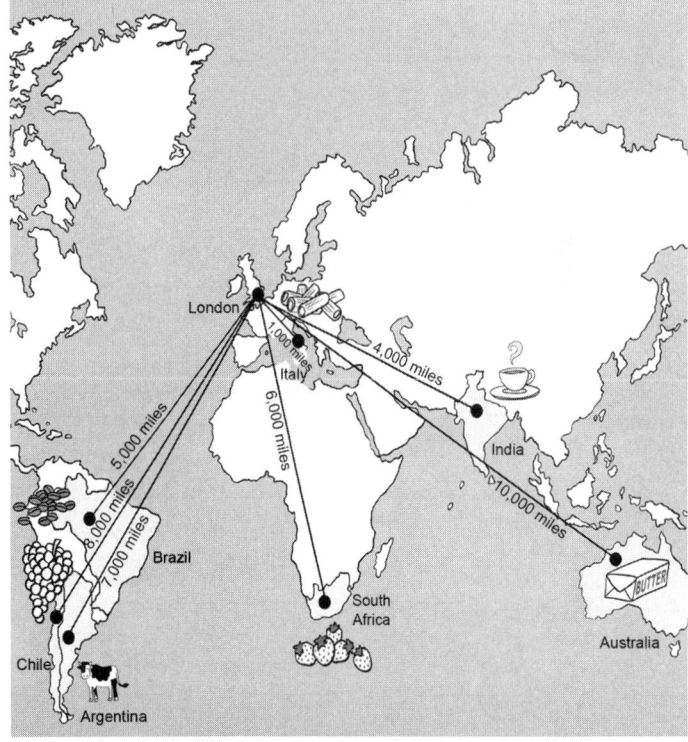

1 grapes   4 strawberries   7 butter
2 beef   5 pasta
3 coffee   6 tea

1 *There are some grapes. They come from Chile. That's about 8,000 miles away.*

Sports

3

Vocabulary: Sports and places

1 ★ Match the sports (1–8) to the places (a–h).

1 basketball	_c_	a) course
2 swimming	___	b) ring
3 skating	___	c) court
4 tennis	___	d) court
5 golf	___	e) pool
6 football	___	f) field
7 boxing	___	g) rink

2 ★★ Write the names of the sports; then write *play*, *go*, or *do*.

1  _go_ ice _skating_ ___

2  ___ s___

3  ___ g___

4  ___ g___

5  ___ t___

6  ___ j___

7  ___ w___

8  ___ c___

9 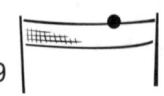 ___ v___

10  ___ k___

Grammar: Verbs of emotion + gerund form (*-ing*)

3 ★ Complete Tom's survey with the correct form of the verbs.

Girls and boys
— the same or different?

Name: Julio Ramirez

What do you think?

Play football

1 I love _playing football_ .

Do gymnastics

2 I hate _____ .

Go swimming

3 I don't mind _____ .

Boys: Think of a girl you know.
Girls: Think of a boy you know.
What does he or she think?

Get dirty

4 [She ▼] hates _____ .

Fall down in the snow

5 [She ▼] doesn't mind _____ .

Watch sports

6 [She ▼] doesn't like _____ .
   She prefers _____ (play) them.

What do your friends think?

Play individual sports

7 They like _____ .

Lose

8 They don't mind _____ ,
   but they prefer _____ (win)!

Listen to music

9 They love _____ .

4 ★★ **Complete the conversation with the correct form of the verbs in parentheses.**

Owen: Hi, Sergio. Where are you going?

Sergio: I'm going to the new tennis courts.

Owen: **1** _Do you like playing_ (you / like / play) tennis?

Sergio: No, I **2** _____ (not), and I **3** (not / enjoy / watch) _____

tennis either. My girlfriend is playing today. What about you?

Owen: I'm going shopping.

Sergio: No! You **4** _____ (hate / go) shopping!

Owen: I know, but I want to buy a ski outfit.

Sergio: **5** _____ (you / like / ski)?

Owen: Oh, yes. I **6** _____ (enjoy / snowboard), too, but I

7 _____ (prefer / ski).

Sergio: My sister **8** _____ (love / go) to the mountains. I **9** _____ (not / like / ski). I **10** _____ (hate / fall) down, and I always fall down when I go skiing.

Owen: I **11** _____ (not / mind / fall) down . . . Aaaaaaaaah! Ow!

Sergio: Are you OK?

Owen: No, I'm not. Help me up.

Sergio: What's wrong? You don't mind falling down!

Owen: I don't mind falling down in the snow.

I **12** _____ (not / like / fall) down on the sidewalk!

Phrases

5 ★ **Circle the correct phrases.**

George: Hey, Maria is on the girl's basketball team.

Pablo: What? Maria hates playing sports! She only likes playing video games.

George: **1** _She's really good at / Great pass /_ (Ha ha!) I know what you mean. She loves chatting online. But it's true—**2** _me, too / she's really good at / ha ha_ basketball.

Pablo: Wow. Is she playing now?

George: Yes, she is. In the gym. Come on. Look! There she is. Maria! Give the ball to Ana. Oh, **3** _great pass / ha ha / me, too_, Maria! Two points for us.

Pablo: Hey, I'm really enjoying this.

George: **4** _She's really good at / Great pass / Me, too_. It's great. We can watch her again next week.

Consolidation

6 **Complete the ad with the words from the box.**

> • courts • doing • don't • go • hate • mind
> • ~~playing~~ • pool • prefer • track

Do you like **1** _playing_ tennis?

Do you enjoy **2** _____ athletics?

Do you **3** _____ swimming every day?

Come to the **Regis Sports Center**.

We have four tennis **4** _____ , an excellent athletics **5** _____ , and an Olympic-sized swimming **6** _____ .

But if you **7** _____ like playing sports, we don't **8** _____ ! We know that some people **9** _____ relaxing, and we **10** _____ seeing unhappy people. That's why we have an Internet café and two movie theaters!

Come to the Regis Sports Center.
It's not just for sports fans!

Vocabulary: Parts of the body

1 ★ Label the pictures.

1 h*air*

2 n_____

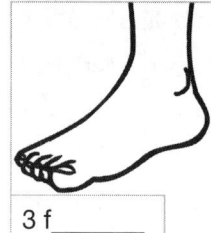
3 f_____

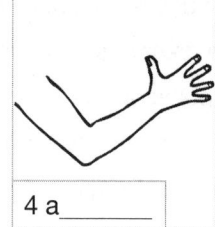
4 a_____

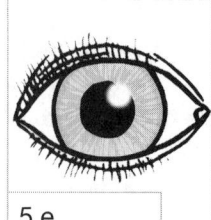
5 e_____

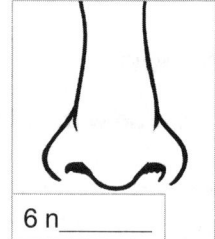
6 n_____

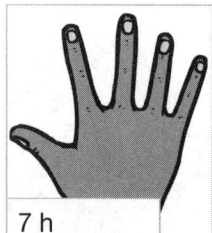
7 h_____

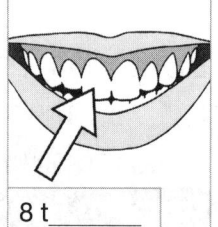
8 t_____

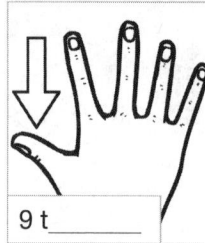
9 t_____

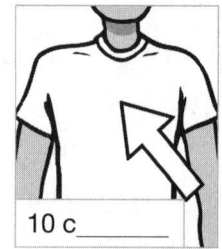
10 c_____

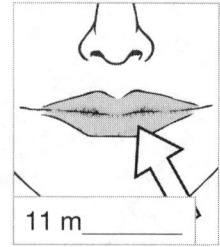
11 m_____

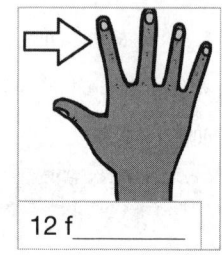
12 f_____

2 ★★ Find nine more parts of the body in the word search and use them to label the picture.

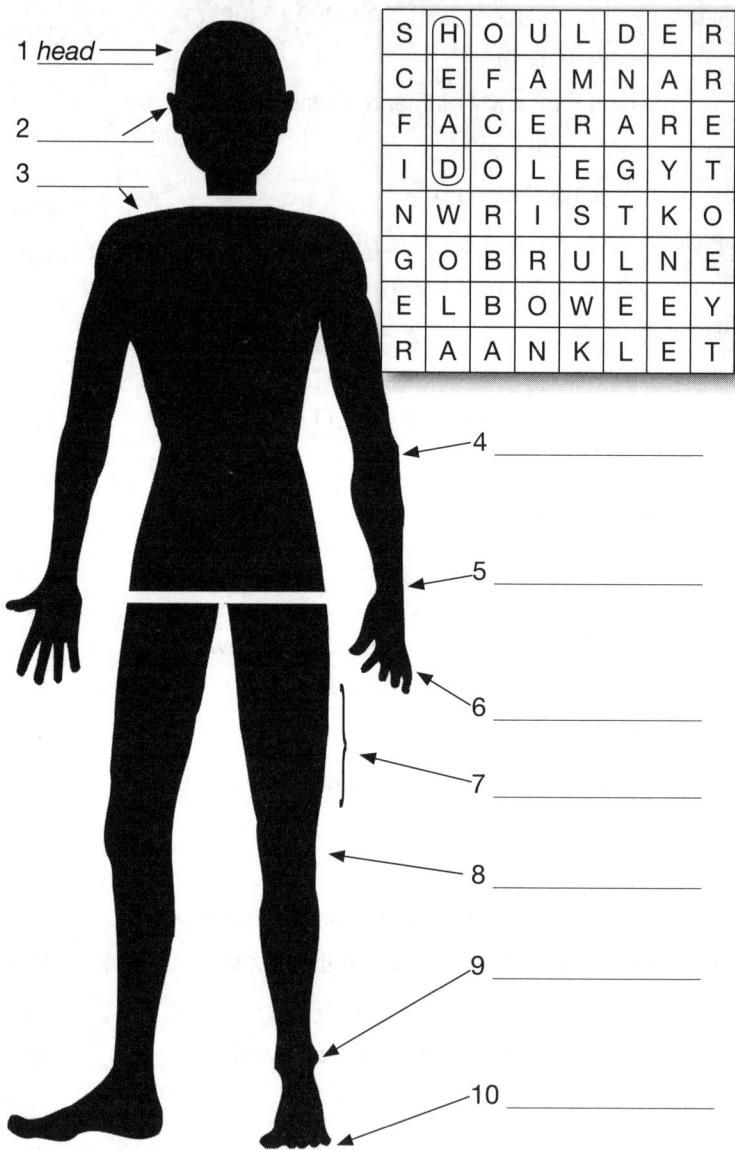

1 *head*
2 _____
3 _____
4 _____
5 _____
6 _____
7 _____
8 _____
9 _____
10 _____

S	H	O	U	L	D	E	R
C	E	F	A	M	N	A	R
F	A	C	E	R	A	R	E
I	D	O	L	E	G	Y	T
N	W	R	I	S	T	K	O
G	O	B	R	U	L	N	E
E	L	B	O	W	E	E	Y
R	A	A	N	K	L	E	T

Grammar: Imperatives

3 ★ Write the correct imperatives.

1 *Don't listen* (listen ✗) to music in the library!

2 Joe! It's seven o'clock! _____ (get ✓) up now!

3 _____ (sit ✗) down on the basketball court!

4 _____ (put ✓) your hand on his shoulder.

5 _____ (touch ✗) the ball with your hands. It's soccer!

6 _____ (look ✓) where you're going! There are a lot of people here.

Grammar: *must/must not* for rules

4 ★ Rewrite the rules using *must* or *must not*.

Kate—some rules for you and your friends while we are out!

For you!

1 Take care of Max.
You must take care of Max.

2 Don't touch your dad's old videos.
You must not touch your dad's old videos.

3 Call us if there's a problem.
_____

4 Don't be noisy.
_____

5 Stay downstairs.
_____

6 Don't eat in the living room.
_____

7 No dancing on the new carpet.
_____

8 Don't go into our bedroom.
_____

For your friends! Tell them to . . .

9 take their shoes off.
_____

10 go home at 11 P.M.
_____

Have a good time! See you at about midnight.
Mom

Consolidation

5 Complete the conversation with the words from the box.

• arm • bend • don't • elbow • fingers • hand
• must • must not • take • thumb • worry • wrist

Doctor: Good morning. What's the problem?

Nick: It's my 1 _____ *arm*. It hurts.

Doctor: Let me take a look. 2 _____ your 3 _____ .

Nick: It's not up there that hurts. It's here.

Doctor: Your 4 _____ ? OK, 5 _____ off your
watch. Now, let me see your 6 _____ . Move
your 7 _____ . Good. And your 8 _____
_____ . I see. Do you play a lot of tennis?

Nick: Yes, I do.

Doctor: 9 _____ play for a month. You 10 _____ give
your hand a rest.

Nick: But there's a school tennis tournament next week.

Doctor: You 11 _____ play. Don't 12 _____ . Here's a
note for your teachers. You must not move your
wrist for the next month, so no homework for you!

Nick: Wow! Great!

Extra challenge!

6 ★★★ Write a set of instructions in your notebook for each sign. Use *must* or *must not*.

1 enter

You must not enter
without a ticket.

2 smoke

_____

3 leave

_____

4 wear

_____

5 park

_____

6 turn off

_____

I'm not going to do that again!

Grammar: *be going to* for future plans, intentions, and predictions

1 ★ Look at the vacation plans and write complete sentences.

Our vacation plans

We:
  1 ✓ *go on vacation by car*
  2 ✗ *stay in a hotel*

I:
  3 ✓ *swim every day*
  4 ✗ *eat a lot*

Sara:
  5 ✓ *buy presents for her friends*
  6 ✗ *worry about school*

Liam:
  7 ✓ *make lots of friends*
  8 ✗ *spend any money*

My parents:
  9 ✓ *send lots of postcards*
  10 ✗ *sunbathe*

1 *We're going to go on vacation by car.*

2 *We aren't going to stay in a hotel.*

3 _____

_____

4 _____

_____

5 _____

_____

6 _____

_____

7 _____

_____

8 _____

_____

9 _____

_____

10 _____

_____

2 ★★ Complete the conversation using the correct form of the verbs in parentheses.

Kelly: Well, classes are over on Friday. Not long to go now.

Ben: I know. It **1** *'s going to be* (be) great!

Kelly: What **2** _____ you _____ (do)?

Ben: First, I **3** _____ (put) all my books away and I **4** _____ (not / look) at them until September.

Kelly: **5** _____ you _____ (go) to Liam's party on Friday?

Ben: No, I **6** _____ (not). My dad **7** _____ (take) me to a basketball game. We **8** _____ (take) the train to Chicago and stay in a hotel.

Kelly: **9** _____ your dad _____ (take) you to a concert on Friday night?

Ben: No, we **10** _____ (not do) anything after the game, but we **11** _____ (go) to the Field Museum on Saturday afternoon.

Kelly: When **12** _____ you _____ (be) home again?

Ben: On Saturday night.

Kelly: See you on Sunday, then.

Ben: OK, great. . . . Uh-oh.

Kelly: What?

Ben: It's nearly ten o'clock. Class starts in five minutes.

3 ★★ Look at the pictures. Write two sentences about what is and isn't going to happen.

1 (rain / not finish this match)

a) *It's going to rain* .

b) *We're not going to finish this game* .

2 (fall down / not go skiing again)

a) Stella _____

_____ .

b) She _____

_____ .

3 (late / not make my flight)

a) I _____

_____ .

b) I _____

_____ .

4 (lose / not get any points)

a) We _____

_____ .

b) We _____

_____ .

5 (upset / not ready by one)

a) Mom _____

_____ .

b) Lunch _____

_____ .

6 (sick / not finish all their food)

a) They _____

_____ .

b) They _____

_____ .

Use your English: Ask for, make, and respond to suggestions

4 ★ Complete the conversations with the correct form of the verbs.

1 **go**

Matt: Why don't we *go* out? Do you want to _____ to the movies?

Brett: No, it's boring. How about _____ swimming?

Matt: Oh, OK. What about _____ to the new pool on Market Road?

Brett: Great idea.

2 **have**

Amy: Do you want to _____ a burger for lunch?

Ella: No, I don't like burgers. Why don't we _____ a barbecue?

Amy: A barbecue? It's going to rain. What about _____ a pizza?

Ella: OK. How about _____ one of my homemade specials?

Amy: Great!

Consolidation

5 Complete the conversation with the words from the box.

• about • do • don't • do you want • feel
• idea • isn't • kidding • what • why

Hector: Hi, Phil. It's Hector. What 1 *do you want* to do today?

Phil: Hi, Hector. I don't know. Why 2 _____ we go to the café?

Hector: No, I don't 3 _____ like it. I want to 4 _____ something outside.

Phil: Outside? It's not a very nice day.

Hector: Don't worry. It 5 _____ going to rain. How 6 _____ doing some skateboarding?

Phil: Skateboarding? You're 7 _____ ! I hate it. I have an idea. 8 _____ don't we play basketball with Sergio and Carlos?

Hector: Yes, that's a great 9 _____ . Where?

Phil: 10 _____ about going to the park?

Hector: OK. See you in about 20 minutes.

INTEGRATED
CONSOLIDATION
SKILLS

Online friends

Before you read

1 Before you read, check the meaning of these words.

> **New words**
> • anyway • coffee shop • computer screen
> • might be • online

Vicki: Hi, Tessa. I'm going out with Maria and Rachel this evening. **1** _d_ ? We're going to have something to eat and then go to the movies.

Tessa: I can't. I'm going to chat with Luisa.

Vicki: **2** _____

Tessa: She's my best friend. You don't know her.

Vicki: **3** _____

Tessa: We chat online. She's great.

Vicki: **4** _____

Tessa: No. She's from Mexico. I really like her, we chat all the time.

Vicki: Come on, Tessa. She's not your real friend. Let's go and have coffee and a cookie.

Tessa: I'm not hungry. Anyway, I want to go to the Internet café. Luisa might be online.

Vicki: Well, I'm going to meet Maria and Rachel at the coffee shop. You know, real people you can talk to. **5** _____

Tessa: Hi, Luisa. **6** _____

Luisa: Hi, Tessa. Yes, I'm here.

Tessa: I'm really upset today. My friends don't understand me. Do you have time to chat later?

Luisa: I'm sorry, but I can't chat tonight. I'm going out with my friends. Talk to you tomorrow.

Read

2 ★ Read the conversation. Then complete the sentences with the correct names.

1 Vicki is going to meet _____ and _____ at the coffee shop.

2 Tessa says her best friend is _____ .

3 Luisa chats with _____ online.

4 Maria and Rachel are going to meet _____ .

3 ★★ Read the conversation again. Show where the questions (a–f) go by writing the numbers (1–6).

a) Who's she? ☐

b) Not just a name on a computer screen. ☐

c) Does she live near here? ☐

d) ~~Do you want to come with us?~~ ☐ _1_

e) Are you there? ☐

f) How do you know her? ☐

Listen

> **Learning strategy: Predict**
> **Remember!** Before you listen, try to predict what is going to happen and what people are going to say. This helps you to understand when you listen.

4 ★ Look at the picture and caption. Use them to figure out answers to the questions.

I'm sorry

1 Who do you think the girl standing is?

   a) Vicki   b) Luisa   c) Tessa

2 Who are the three girls sitting down?

   a) Luisa, Vicki, and Tessa

   b) Vicki, Maria, and Rachel

   c) Tessa, Luisa, and Maria

3 Who do you think is sorry?

   a) Tessa   b) Vicki   c) Luisa

5 ★ (4) Listen and check your answers to Exercise 4.

6 ★★ (4) Listen again and decide who says these things. Write *V* (*Vicki*) or *T* (*Tessa*).

1 Hey, don't cry.	V
2 Do you still like me?	
3 Come on, smile!	
4 Do you want some coffee?	
5 I'm going to have a cookie.	
6 We're going to go out for Chinese food.	
7 I love going out.	
8 Internet friendships are the worst!	

Write

7 ★ Look at this information. On a piece of paper, write a message to Nicola telling her your plans for Friday and Saturday (What are they?) and suggest a different time to chat. (When?)

- You have an online friend. Her name is Nicola.
- She wants to spend Friday night chatting with you online and sending you photos.
- You have plans for Friday. You're going to go out with your friends.
- On Saturday, you're also going to be busy.

Start like this:

Hi, Nicola,
Thanks for your message. I'm sorry, but . . .

Places

It's larger than our house.

Vocabulary: Home and furniture

1 ★ Label the parts of the home.

1 *chimney*

2 r_____

3 a_____

4 b_____

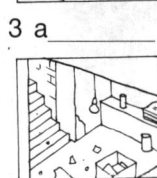

5 b_____

2 ★★ Complete the paragraph with the words from the box.

• ceiling • fence • gate • stairs • yard

We have a beautiful old house. You can't see it from the road because there's a very high **1** *fence* all the way around it. You go in through a small **2** _____ , and you're in the **3** _____ . It's full of trees and flowers. It's very beautiful. In the house, there's a kitchen on the left and a living room on the right. You go up the **4** _____ , and there are two bedrooms and one other room. The rooms are all small. I can touch the **5** _____ in my bedroom!

Grammar: Comparative and superlative forms of adjectives

3 ★ Look at the information and complete the sentences using the comparative and superlative forms of the adjectives.

My father is 6 feet 2 inches, my mother is 5 feet 8 inches, and my sister is 5 feet 3 inches.

tall/short

1 My father is *taller than* my mother.

2 My sister is *the shortest* person in my family.

3 My father is _____ person in my family.

4 My mother is _____ my father.

The white car costs $5,000, the gray car costs $20,000, and the black car costs $40,000.

cheap/expensive

5 The white car is _____ of all the cars.

6 The gray car is _____ the white car.

7 The white car is _____ the black car.

8 The black car is _____ of all the cars.

My house is 400 square feet, Jake's house is 800 square feet, and Chris's house is 1,500 square feet.

big/small

9 My house is _____ Jake's house.

10 Chris's house is _____ Jake's house.

11 My house is _____ of the three houses.

12 Chris's house is _____ of the three houses.

4

4 ★★ Complete the letter. Write one word in each blank.

Dear Nicola,

Here's a photo of my new house. It's great! It's **1** _more modern_
than (modern) our old house. There are three bedrooms. Mom
and Dad's bedroom is **2** _____ _____ (big), of course!
My bedroom is **3** _____ _____ (small), but I don't mind
because I have a balcony. The yard is **4** _____ _____
(nice) our old yard. The flowers are **5** _____ _____
_____ (beautiful) the flowers we had there.
The attic is **6** _____ _____ _____ (exciting) thing
about the house. It's amazing! We have a basement, too,
but I think the attic is **7** _____ _____ (good) the
basement. I go up there every day. I like it because it's
8 _____ _____ (quiet) the rest of the house, and I can
think there. **9** _____ _____ (bad) thing about the house is
that it's **10** _____ (far) from school _____ our old house.
It takes about 30 minutes to walk to school now.
Hope you can come and see it soon!
Love,
Rebecca

Consolidation

5 Complete the sentences using the cues.

My mom

1 good / ▨ / beautiful

The best place is _the yard_ because it is _the most_
beautiful place to sit.

2 bad / ▨ / cold

The worst place is _the basement_ because it is _the_
coldest place in the house.

My dad

3 useful / ▨ / big

_____ room is
_____ because it is _____
room in the house.

4 annoying / ▨ / difficult

_____ place is
_____ because it is _____
place to keep clean and neat.

Me

5 good / ▨ / warm

_____ place is
_____ because it is _____
place to sunbathe.

6 nice / ▨ / quiet

_____ room is _____
because it is _____ room in the house.

My sister

7 boring / ▨ / empty

_____ room is _____
because it is _____ room.

8 bad / ▨ / small

_____ place is _____
because it is _____ place and
there's no room for her!

27

There isn't much room.

Vocabulary: Common noncount nouns

1 ★ Look at the pictures and complete the words.

1 *time* _____

2 f_____

3 l_____

4 m_____

5 m_____

6 f_____

7 h_____

8 g_____

9 t_____

2 ★★ Add one word from the box to each group.

> • armchair • backpack • bicycles • broken glass
> • days • MP3 files • practice tests • tomatoes • ~~$20~~

1 dollars, coins, 10¢, *$20*

2 desk, chair, sofa, _____

3 hours, seconds, minutes, _____

4 wastepaper, old batteries, empty candy wrappers,

_____

5 suitcase, bags, _____

6 motorcycles, cars, trucks, _____

7 potatoes, carrots, hot dogs, _____

8 exercises, projects, _____

9 CDs, songs, radio, _____

Grammar: Count and noncount nouns with *much, many, a lot of, a few, a little*

3 ★ Circle the correct words.

1 I don't have *many /* (much) money.

2 I have *a lot of / much* homework to do.

3 We still have *a little / few* time. Don't worry.

4 We don't have *much / many* CDs.

5 How *much / many* exercises do we have for homework?

6 You have *much / a lot of* luggage.

7 There are a *few / little* eggs here.

8 There isn't *much / many* traffic on our street. It's very quiet.

4 ★★ Look at the pictures. Write sentences using the cues and the words from the box.

> • CDs • chairs • dollars • furniture • ~~luggage~~
> • minutes • money • music • ~~suitcases~~ • time

1 a lot of / a lot of

He has *a lot of luggage.*

He has *a lot of suitcases.*

2 much / many

They don't have _____

_____

They don't have _____

_____

3 a few / a little

There are _____

_____

There's _____

_____

4 much / many

There isn't _____

_____ before

the train leaves.

There aren't _____

_____ before

the train leaves.

5 a little / a few

They have _____

_____

They have _____

_____

Use your English: Ask permission and respond

5 ★ Complete the second conversation so that it means the same as the first one.

1 A: Can I use your bike?   B: Sure.

　A: May *I use* your bike?

　B: *Yes,* certainly.

2 A: Can I listen to some music?   B: Sure.

　A: _____ _____ OK _____ _____ listen to

　　some music?

　B: Yes, of _____ .

3 A: May I borrow that book?   B: Yes, certainly.

　A: _____ _____ all right _____ _____

　　borrow that book?

　B: No _____ !

4 A: Can I borrow $5?   B: Sorry, no.

　A: May _____ _____ $5?

　B: _____ , I don't have any money. Sorry.

Consolidation

6 Complete the three conversations with the words from the box.

> • Actually • ~~can~~ • course • few • lot • many
> • much • much • much • much

Ben:　Jack, **1** *can* I borrow a **2** _____ CDs for our party?

Jack:　Yes, of **3** _____ . There's a lot of rock, but there

　　　　isn't **4** _____ rap. The CDs are over there.

Ben:　Thanks!

Vicki:　Mom, I don't have **5** _____ money left. Can I

　　　　have my allowance early this week?

Mom: **6** _____ , not right now. I'm going to

　　　　the bank later. How **7** _____ do you want?

Todd:　Can I borrow your dictionary?

Josh:　Sorry, I need it. I have a **8** _____ of

　　　　homework to do.

Todd:　How **9** _____ exercises do you have?

Josh:　I don't know, but I don't have **10** _____ time!

Phrases

1 ★ Complete the phrases by writing one letter in each blank.

1 A: They're going to build a new shopping center in town. It's going to have stores and lots of other things.

  B: Wow! It s o u n d s g r e a t!

2 A: Our class is going on a trip to Vancouver next month.

  B: R _ _ l l y? T h _ _'s
  _ n t _ r _ s _ _ n g.

3 A: What's on TV tonight?

  B: So _ _ y. I d _ _ 't h _ _ _
  a c l _ _. I never watch TV.

4 A: Can I borrow a pen?
  B: OK.
  A: Can I use your dictionary?
  B: Yes. Here you are.
  A: Do you have some paper?
  B: G _ v _ me a b r _ _ k! I'm trying to do my homework.

Vocabulary: Large numbers

2 ★ Write the numbers in words.

1 **120** *one hundred and twenty*

2 **265** two _____ _____
_____-five

3 **501** _____ _____
and _____

4 **1,150** one _____ , one
_____ ____ _____

5 **10,746** _____ thousand, _____
hundred ____ _____-_____

6 **152,381** one _____ and
_____-_____ thousand,
_____ and
_____-_____

Grammar: Question word *how* + adjectives of dimension

3 ★ Complete the blanks (1–7) in the conversation with the questions (a–g).

a) How heavy is the statue?
b) How tall is it?
c) How long is the statue's finger?
d) How big is Ellis Island?
e) ~~How old is the statue?~~
f) How far is it from Liberty Island to Ellis Island?
g) How many steps do we climb to get to the top of the statue?

Tour guide: Good afternoon, everyone. Welcome to our tour of the Statue of Liberty and Ellis Island. Our first stop today is Liberty Island and the Statue of Liberty. The boat ride will take about 20 minutes. Does anyone have any questions?

Tourist 1: Yes. **1** *How old is the statue?*

Tour guide: About 130 years old. The French government gave it to the United States in 1886.

Tourist 2: **2** _____

Tour guide: From the base to the tip of the torch, it's about 305 feet, or 93 meters tall. The arm is 42 feet, or 13 meters long!

Tourist 2: Oh, really? **3** _____

Tour guide: Her finger? Her index finger is 8 feet, or 3 meters long.

Tourist 2: **4** _____

Tour guide: Well, it's made out of copper and steel, so it's pretty heavy! It weighs 450,000 pounds, or 200,000 kilos!

Tourist 2: **5** _____

Tour guide: Well, there are 354 steps to climb up to the crown of the statue. But we can't go up there today. Sorry. You can visit the lobby. After that, we're going to Ellis Island.

Tourist 2: Oh. **6** _____

Tour guide: Not far at all . . . the islands are very close.

Tourist 3: **7** _____

Tour guide: It's 32 acres, or 130,000 square meters. It's a lot bigger than Liberty Island.

4 ★★ Answer the questions using the information from Exercise 3. Check (✓) *True*, *False*, or *No information*.

	True	False	No information
1 The Statue of Liberty is 1,886 years old.		✓	
2 The Statue is 305 feet high.			
3 The Statue's arm is 8 feet long.			
4 The Statue weighs 400,000 pounds.			
5 Liberty Island is about 10 acres.			
6 Ellis Island is 32 acres.			

Consolidation

5 Read the two profiles and complete the descriptions.

Places to visit in Europe

1 Height of mountain: 12,460 feet (3,798 meters)
Length of road: 30 miles (47.8 kilometers)
Height of road: 9,029 feet (2,572 meters)

The Grossglockner High Alpine Road is one of Europe's most beautiful roads. It is nearly 30 miles **1** *long* and reaches a height of nine **2** _____ , and twenty-nine feet. The mountain, though, is twelve thousand, **3** _____ hundred and sixty feet **4** _____ high.

2 Length: 10 miles (16 kilometers)
Most famous part (The Iron Gates): width 13 feet (4 meters); height of sides 1,640 feet (500 meters)
Distance from Athens: 112 miles (180 kilometers)

The Samaria Gorge on the island of Crete is a beautiful place to walk. It is 10 miles **5** _____ , but most people remember one small section called The Iron Gates. Here, the gorge is only 13 feet **6** _____ , while the sides are 1,640 feet **7** _____ . How **8** _____ is Crete from Athens? It's about one hundred **9** _____ twelve miles away.

Extra challenge!

6 ★★★ Complete the questions. Then circle the correct answers.

1 *How high* is it?
It's 1,063 feet high. It's . . .
(a) the Eiffel Tower.
b) the Empire State Building.
c) the Burj Khalifa.

2 _____ is it?
It's 4,000 miles long. It's . . .
a) the Amazon River.
b) the Mississippi River.
c) the Danube River.

3 _____ are they?
They weigh about 0.03 pounds.
They are . . .
a) laptops.
b) CDs.
c) cell phones.

4 _____ is it?
At its deepest, it is 8,202 feet deep.
It's the . . .
a) Red Sea.
b) Pacific Ocean.
c) North Sea.

5 _____ is it? It is about 60 to 100 feet wide. It's the . . .
a) the Panama Canal.
b) the Thames River in London.
c) the Grand Canal in Venice.

6 _____ is it from New York City?
It's about 3,629 miles. It's . . .
a) Miami, Florida
b) Mexico City, Mexico
c) Lima, Peru

INTEGRATED SKILLS

CONSOLIDATION

Movie locations

Before you read

1 Before you read, check the meaning of these words.

> **New words**
> • arched • domes • fountains • iron (n)
> • market • stalls • stunt person

Read

2 ★ Read the article and match the places (1–4) to the movies (a–d).

1 Bellagio Hotel _c_
2 Leadenhall Market ____
3 Eden Project ____
4 Flatiron building ____

a) *Tomb Raider* ____
b) *Spider Man* ____
c) *Ocean's Eleven* ____
d) *Die Another Day* ____

The giant Bellagio Hotel in Las Vegas is now 12 years old. The hotel's name comes from the town of Bellagio on Lake Como in Italy. The hotel has its own lake with fountains that are a major tourist attraction. It is famous as the hotel that Andy Garcia owns in *Ocean's Eleven*, *Twelve*, and *Thirteen*. There are 3,933 bedrooms in the hotel!

Leadenhall Market in London is a beautiful market. It is covered with an arched roof. It is more than 130 years old. The arched roof is an amazing sight and it is a popular tourist attraction. There are lots of stalls in the market. They sell fresh meat, fruit, and fish. It is popular as a place to film, too. Angelina Jolie rides a motorcycle through the market in *Tomb Raider*.

BUILDINGS IN THE MOVIES

The ten-year-old Eden Project in Cornwall in the U.K. is an awesome sight. There are several giant, steel domes. There are plants from all over the world. The acoustics inside the domes are perfect for concerts. In the James Bond movie *Die Another Day*, Halle Berry (or a stunt person) climbed down one of the domes.

The 100-year-old Flatiron building in New York got its name because of its shape. It looks like an iron. It is 285 feet (87 meters) high, with 22 floors. At one end, it is about 82 feet (25 meters) wide, but at the other, it is only 7 feet (2 meters) across. In movies, it is the home of the *Daily Bugle* newspaper in the *Spider-Man* movies.

3 ★★ **Read the article again and write the names of the places. Write BH (Bellagio Hotel), LM (Leadenhall Market), EP (Eden Project), or FB (Flatiron building).**

1 It's the oldest building.   *LM*

2 It's a good place for concerts.   ____

3 Its name is also the name of a town.   ____

4 It's the most modern building.   ____

5 You can buy fresh food here.   ____

6 Its name comes from its shape.   ____

7 You can sleep in one of 3,933 bedrooms here. ____

8 This building has its own lake.   ____

9 There are plants from all over the world here. ____

10 The article gives the height of this building. ____

Listen

4 ★ 🎧 **5 Listen to a tour guide at Alnwick Castle in England and complete the information.**

1 The oldest parts of the castle are nearly *one thousand* years old.

2 Most of the castle on the tour is about two _____

_____ .

3 There are _____ square feet of gardens.

4 More than half a _____ visitors come here each year.

5 The castle is in the _____ movies.

6 The castle opens on March _____ .

7 It closes again on the 26th of _____ .

8 The gardens open at _____ each day.

9 The castle opens one hour _____ than the gardens.

Write

> **Writing tip: Conjunctions *but* and *however***
> **Remember!** We can join two contrasting ideas with *but*. We can also use *however*.
> *But* can join two sentences. It follows a comma.
> *It moves all the time, **but** it goes very slowly.*
> *However* usually comes first in a sentence and is followed by a comma.
> *It's in the west of London. **However**, you can see it from the center.*

5 ★ **Rewrite the sentences using *but* or *however*.**

1 Some parts of the castle are 1,000 years old, but most of it is about 200 years old. (however)

Some parts of the castle are 1,000 years old.

However, most of it is about two hundred years old.

2 One end of the Flatiron building is 82 feet wide, but the other end is only 7 feet wide. (however)

_____

_____

3 In *Die Another Day*, Halle Berry's character climbs the Eden Project. However, it isn't really her. (but)

_____

_____

4 The gardens at Alnwick open at 10 A.M. However, the castle doesn't open until 11 A.M. (but)

_____

_____

6 ★★ **Read. Then write a paragraph using *but* and *however* at least once each.**

The Empire State Building

Height: 1,453 feet   **Floors:** 102
Age: 80 years old   **Visitors:** 4 million a year

Movies: *King Kong* (climbs it and falls off it), *Independence Day* (aliens destroy it), *Sleepless in Seattle* (Tom Hanks meets Meg Ryan at the top)

Highest building in New York—NOT in the U.S. (Willis Tower in Chicago is higher)
Most popular tourist attraction in New York—NOT in the U.S. (Disney World, Florida is more popular)

Were you in my room?

Phrases

1 ★ **Match the sentences (1–4) to the replies (a–d).**

1 What's on TV tonight? _a_

2 Hi, Jack. Where are you? Are you still on vacation? __

3 Pete is the best tennis player in the world. __

4 Do you have my cell phone? __

a) Dunno.

b) Of course not! It's probably in your bag.

c) No, I'm back. I'm at the train station.

d) You're crazy. My little sister is better than he is.

Vocabulary: Dates

2 ★ **Match the dates (1–8) to the correct words (a–h).**

1 1/18/1871 ___d___

2 8/15/1916 __

3 11/11/2000 __

4 5/4/1961 __

5 10/15/1619 __

6 7/18/1817 __

7 12/11/2001 __

8 4/5/1960 __

a) the eleventh of November, two thousand

b) the fourth of May, nineteen sixty-one

c) the fifteenth of October, sixteen nineteen

d) the eighteenth of January, eighteen seventy-one

e) the eleventh of December, two thousand and one

f) the fifth of April, nineteen sixty

g) the eighteenth of July, eighteen seventeen

h) the fifteenth of August, nineteen sixteen

Grammar: Simple past of verb *be*

3 ★ **Complete Toby's e-mail with *was*, *wasn't*, *were*, or *weren't*.**

| From: | Toby |
| To: | Jake |

Hi, Jake,

How are you? I'm back in Seattle now. I **1** _was_ in Mexico last week with friends. We **2** _____ in Mexico City, Veracruz, and Monterrey. Mexico City **3** _____ great. Unfortunately, the weather **4** _____ very good, but the city is fantastic. We **5** _____ in a hotel because they are kind of expensive. We **6** _____ in a youth hostel instead. The restaurants **7** _____ pretty good, but the restaurants in Veracruz **8** _____ better.

Send me an e-mail soon.

Toby

4 ★★ Look at the factfile. Write questions and answers using *was*, *wasn't*, *were*, or *weren't*.

ZAC EFRON

Born:	October 18, 1987, in San Luis Obispo, California
Mother:	Starla, administrative assistant
Father:	David, engineer
Brother:	Dylan
First TV show:	*Firefly*
First big role:	Troy Bolton in *High School Musical*
Girlfriend:	Vanessa Hudgens (co-star in *High School Musical*)

1 (When / born?) *When was he born?*
   He was born on October 18, 1987.

2 (Where / born?) _____
   _____

3 (parents / actors?) _____
   _____

4 (What / first TV show?) _____
   _____

5 (What / first big role?) _____
   _____

6 (he / in a movie with his girlfriend?)
   _____
   _____

Grammar: Past adverbial phrases

5 ★ Complete the sentences with *last* or *yesterday*.

1 Where were you *last* _____ Saturday?

2 There was a great movie on TV _____ night.

3 I was very tired _____ night.

4 That was my favorite movie _____ year.

5 Why weren't you at school _____ afternoon?

6 Were you late for school _____ morning?

Consolidation

6 Complete the conversation with the correct past form of *be* or the preposition *in* or *on*.

Emma: Can you help me with this quiz? When **1** *was* Elvis Presley born?

Andy: I don't know. I **2** _____ born then!

Emma: Come on. **3** _____ it **4** _____ 1935, 1950, or 1965?

Andy: I think it **5** _____ 1935. My grandparents **6** _____ born in the 1930s, and they **7** _____ big Elvis fans.

Emma: **8** _____ they interested in rock music?

Andy: Yes, they **9** _____ .

Emma: Cool. My grandparents **10** _____ . They **11** _____ only interested in classical music. OK. Here's the next question. When **12** _____ John Lennon born?

Andy: Oh, I know that. I love the Beatles. He was born **13** _____ October 9, 1940.

Emma: Wow! Thanks.

Vocabulary: Common regular verbs

1 ★ Circle the correct verbs.

1 How often do you *talk* / *ask* to Michelle in the morning?

2 Are you going to *answer* / *reply* that text message?

3 Do you *remember* / *realize* your fifth birthday?

4 Can you just *decide* / *pick* one dessert, please?

5 We always *arrive* / *stay* at the same hotel there.

6 The class *starts* / *arrives* at seven o'clock.

7 Lucy *looks* / *likes* really good in that hat.

8 Be careful! Don't *drop* / *turn* that glass.

9 When I'm busy, I don't *hurry* / *notice* the time.

10 Help me. I can't *decide* / *order* what to wear!

Grammar: Simple past of regular verbs

2 ★ Complete the story with the simple past of the verbs in parentheses.

This **1** *happened* (happen) about three years ago. I was on a busy train. There were no seats. I **2** _____ (open) a pack of gum. I **3** _____ (call) my friend. I **4** _____ (start) talking to him, but the chewing gum **5** _____ (drop) out of my mouth and **6** _____ (land) on a woman's head. She **7** _____ (not notice) at first. I quickly **8** _____ (try) to pick the gum out of her hair. She suddenly **9** _____ (ask): "What are you doing?" I was scared and I **10** _____ (not answer). Luckily, the train **11** _____ (stop) at a station, and I **12** _____ (jump) off quickly. Now I never chew gum on a train!

3 ★ Look at the pictures and write positive or negative sentences using the cues.

Yesterday, David and Alison were in the park.

1 They / want / to go to the zoo   *They wanted to go to the zoo.* _____

2 David / drop / his cell phone   _____

3 Alison / shout / at him   _____

4 David / pick / up his camera   _____

5 Alison / wait / for David   _____

4 ★★ **Write questions and short answers about the people in Exercise 3.**

1 Alison and David / want to go to the zoo?

Did Alison and David want to go to the zoo?

Yes, they did.

2 Alison / drop her camera?

_____

_____

3 David / pick up the camera?

_____

_____

4 David / shout at Alison?

_____

_____

5 Alison / wait for David?

_____

_____

6 Alison and David / arrive at the zoo together?

_____

_____

Consolidation

5 **Complete the conversations with the correct simple past form of the verbs from the box.**

Conversation 1

• call • ~~decide~~ • drop • land • not stop

Mrs. Ortega: Melanie! Why are you so late?

Melanie: My bus was late, so I **1** *decided*

to go by train, but the train **2** _____

at my station.

Mrs. Ortega: **3** _____ you _____ the school office?

Melanie: No, I didn't. I **4** _____

my cell phone in the street, and it

5 _____ under a bus.

Mrs. Ortega: Oh, really? So why is your phone

ringing now, Melanie?

Conversation 2

• arrive • call • end • listen • not want • stay • watch

Phil: I **6** _____ you yesterday afternoon, but you

weren't at home.

Gary: I was at a basketball game at school.

It **7** _____ at six o'clock, and I

8 _____ home at about seven.

Phil: **9** _____ you _____ that new show on TV?

Gary: No, I didn't. I **10** _____

to watch TV yesterday. I **11** _____

in my room and I **12** _____ to music.

Extra challenge!

6 ★★★ **Complete the questions in the quiz. Then match them to the correct answers.**

1 *Did* Christopher Columbus *arrive* in India in 1492? *d*

2 What _____ Pablo Picasso d_____ in 1855? ___

3 _____ Hiram Bingham d_____ Machu Picchu in 1901? ___

4 _____ Eva Peron w_____ as a beautician in the 1940s? ___

5 Why _____ Madonna d_____ to move to Paris? ___

a) No. He discovered it in 1911.

b) She didn't. She moved to London.

c) No. She worked as an actress.

d) No. He arrived in the West Indies.

e) Nothing. He wasn't born yet!

Grammar: Simple past of irregular verbs

1 ★ Find nine verbs in the simple past form in the puzzle. Write the past forms and the base forms.

Z	N	A	T	O	L	D	J	O	E
S	B	R	B	E	I	K	F	Y	C
T	O	O	K	R	M	G	L	E	A
Q	U	C	J	S	T	A	L	D	M
P	G	A	V	E	A	D	M	L	E
X	H	I	L	D	P	I	A	D	P
U	T	V	F	H	A	D	C	E	J
B	R	O	N	G	W	A	G	T	Y
Z	F	E	L	L	U	E	O	P	S
G	C	T	A	L	E	F	T	E	D

1 *told – tell*

2 b_____

3 c_____

4 t_____

5 g_____

6 d_____

7 h_____

8 g_____

9 f_____

10 l_____

2 ★ Complete the conversation with the correct simple past form of the verbs in parentheses.

Greg: What **1** *did* you *do* (do) last weekend?

Ana: We **2** _____ (not do) much. My sister **3** _____ (make) a cake and I **4** _____ (buy) a new shirt. What **5** _____ you _____ (do)?

Greg: We **6** _____ (go) to Portland yesterday.

Ana: Cool. How long **7** _____ it _____ (take) to get there?

Greg: It **8** _____ (not take) long. We **9** _____ (leave) home at eight and **10** _____ (get) there at noon. We **11** _____ (have) lunch at the zoo.

Ana: What **12** _____ you _____ (have)? Hamburgers and french fries?

Greg: No, sandwiches. It was great.

Ana: Hey, next time, you can ask me to come!

Greg: No problem.

3 ★★ Complete the message with the correct form of verbs from the box.

• buy • fall • get up • ~~go~~ • go • have • lose • meet • not do • not like • not listen • take

Sophie: Hi Carlos! How was your weekend? **1** *Did* you *go* to the concert in the park? I **2** _____ anything special. On Saturday, I **3** _____ late and then I **4** _____ shopping. I **5** _____ Shakira's new CD. I was silly, because I **6** _____ to it in the store. When I played it at home, I **7** _____ it, so I **8** _____ it back to the store. Then guess who I **9** _____ downtown? Danny! We **10** _____ coffee together in the new Internet café. It was great to see him again. But there was one problem. I **11** _____ my house key. I think it **12** _____ out of my pocket in the café. My mom wasn't happy with me! Bye for now!

Grammar: Past adverbial phrases with *ago*

4 ★ Rewrite the sentences with *ago*.

1 I saw a movie last Saturday.

   I saw a movie *a week ago* .

2 The test started at ten o'clock.

   The test started _____ .

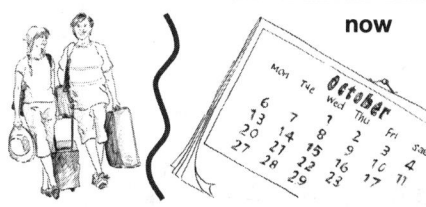

3 We went on vacation in August.

   We went on vacation _____ .

4 I was born in 1994.

   I was born _____ .

5 We had a math test on Monday.

   We had a math test _____ .

6 I arrived here at eight o'clock this morning.

   I arrived here _____ .

Vocabulary: Verb and noun collocations

5 ★ Complete the paragraph with the correct verbs.

Yesterday, I got up late. Then I **1** m*ade* some pancakes. I decided to **2** d_____ my homework before I went to meet my friends. Then I **3** l_____ my bus pass. I couldn't find it anywhere. Of course, I was late and I **4** m_____ my bus. It took an hour to walk into town and I didn't get there until two o'clock. When I **5** t_____ the story to my friends, they didn't believe me.

Use your English: Make and respond to apologies

6 ★ Circle the correct phrases.

Laura: Hi, Nina. Do you have my CD?

Nina: **1** Oh, (sorry) / never mind, it's at home.

Laura: **2** What happened / That's OK. Bring it tomorrow.

Nina: OK. Oh, by the way, here's your notebook.
        3 It doesn't matter / I'm very sorry it's so dirty.

Laura: **4** What happened? / Believe it or not.

Nina: Well, **5** believe it or not / never mind, my dog started to eat it.

Laura: **6** Don't worry / I'm sorry. **7** I'm really sorry / It doesn't matter. I can get a new one at school tomorrow.

Consolidation

7 Complete the conversation with the words from the box. Put the verbs in the simple past form.

> • ago • do • go • last • ~~leave~~ • like • miss
> • not come • not sleep • see • see • take

Julian: Hi. I'm sorry I'm late. I **1** *left* the house two hours **2** _____ , but I **3** _____ the bus and the next bus **4** _____ for an hour!

Mike: Don't worry. Do you want a drink of water?

Julian: Thanks. So, what **5** _____ you _____ last night?

Mike: My brother **6** _____ me to the movies.

Julian: Cool. What **7** _____ you _____ ?

Mike: We **8** _____ *The Eye*.

Julian: I **9** _____ to see that **10** _____ week. **11** _____ you _____ it?

Mike: Yes, it was great, but I **12** _____ that night!

INTEGRATED **CONSOLIDATION** SKILLS

The gold rush

Before you read

1 **Before you read, check the meaning of these words.**

New words
• bear (*n*) • covered • land (*n*) • ox / oxen
• pioneer (*n*) • pull • wagon

The long journey west

In the 1880s, many people left their homes in the east of the United States and went to Oregon and California in the American West. Some went to look for gold, but many were farmers. They wanted land and a better life.

They traveled in covered wagons. Oxen pulled the wagons, because they were strong and didn't eat a lot of food. The journey took many months, and life was hard. When the pioneers arrived at the end of their journey, their new lives as farmers in the West began.

<u>August 14th, 1853</u>
We got up at 4 A.M. today. Mother made breakfast—we had coffee and biscuits. We started the 14th day of our journey at 7 A.M. We didn't walk very fast, because the oxen were tired after a very long day yesterday. I looked for some fruit with my friends. We didn't find any fruit, but we spotted a brown bear in the forest! It ran away through the trees when it saw us.
After lunch, we arrived at a big river. Luckily, the water wasn't deep, so we got across without any problems. We stayed by the river that night. Before I went to sleep, I remembered my old home in the East, but I wasn't sad. I knew I had a new life now.

Jake Hall was a boy who traveled to Oregon with his family. This is an excerpt from his diary.

Read

> **Learning strategy: Scan for specific information**
>
> **Remember!** When you scan a text, don't read from start to finish. Just look for the information you want (a name, a date).

2 ★ Scan the text quickly and find the following information.

1 a country: _the United States_

2 two kinds of animals: _____ , _____

3 two states in the U.S.: _____ , _____

4 a date: _____

5 two kinds of food: _____ , _____

3 ★★ Read the article again. Answer the questions.

1 Where did people want to go to start a new life?

To the American West. / To California and Oregon.

2 Why did oxen pull the wagons?

_____

3 When did Jake's family start their journey?

_____

4 What time did Jake's family start on the 14th day?

_____

5 Why did they walk slowly that day?

_____

6 What did Jake see in the forest?

_____

7 What did it do?

_____

8 Where did Jake and his family stay that night?

_____

9 Was Jake sad? Why?

_____

Listen

4 ★ 🎧 6 When the Hall family finally arrived in Oregon City, a newspaper reporter talked to them. Listen and answer the questions.

1 When did they leave their hometown?

Four months ago, on August 1st.

2 What did they eat on the journey?

_____

3 Was the journey difficult?

_____

4 Why were they tired?

_____

5 Did the children go to school?

_____

6 Why wasn't this a problem?

_____

7 What happened to Mrs. Hall while crossing a river?

_____

8 What woke Jake up one night?

_____

Write

5 ★ Read your answers to Exercise 4. On a piece of paper, write a newspaper article about the Hall family. Start and finish like this:

The Hall family's long journey

The Hall family left their home four months ago on August 1. It was a long journey, but they had no problems with food. They usually ate . . .

The family was happy when they arrived in Oregon City yesterday. At last, they could have a warm bath!

Was she driving?

Phrases

1 ★ Use a phrase from the box that means the same as the underlined words.

> • Guess who! • I wish! • No way!

1 **Lee:** Do you have a ticket for the concert?

   Ed: <u>No, but I'd like to have one.</u> *I wish!*

2 **Matt:** I'm in Beyoncé's new video!

   Jack: I don't believe it. <u>You're kidding</u>.

           _____

3 I met a famous rock star last night. <u>Do you know who?</u> _____

Grammar: Past continuous

2 ★ Complete the sentences with the verbs in parentheses in the past continuous.

Last Saturday, we were very busy. In the morning, . . .

1 I *was doing* (do) my homework.

2 My parents _____ (shop).

3 My sister _____ (chat) with her friends online.

4 My grandparents _____ (drive) to our house.

At two o'clock in the afternoon, . . .

5 I _____ (make) coffee for everyone.

6 My sister and my mom _____ (cook).

7 My grandmother _____ (sleep).

At five o'clock in the afternoon, . . .

8 We _____ (have) a snack.

At six o'clock in the evening, . . .

9 My parents and my grandmother _____ _____ (watch) TV.

10 My grandfather _____ (try) to send an e-mail on my computer!

3 ★★ Look at the information and complete the interview below.

Interview with Donna Fisher—notes

6:00–6:45 *Restaurant: Donna—fish, Louisa—salad, Kelly—chicken*

6:45–7:00 *Walk to movie theater*

7:00–8:45 *Watch "The Duchess". Very good!*

8:45 *Go to party*

9:00–11:00 *At party. Donna—dance, Louisa—talk, Kelly—read a book*

11:00 *Call her dad*

11:15 *Dad arrived—took Kelly and Louisa home.*

12:00 *Asleep!*

A Saturday with Donna Fisher

Last Sunday, I interviewed the teenage singer Donna Fisher.

Me: Donna, can I ask you what you were doing last night?

Donna: Of course.

Me: **1** What <u>were you doing</u> at 6:15?

Donna: I was with my friends. We **2** <u>were eating</u> in a restaurant. I had fish.

Me: **3** Where _____ at 6:50?

Donna: **4** We _____ . We got there at about 7:00.

Me: **5** What _____ at 8:00?

Donna: **6** We _____ The Duchess. It was a very good movie. It ended at about 8:45. Then we went to a party.

Me: **7** What _____ at the party?

Donna: **8** I _____ ; my friend Louisa _____ ; and my other friend, Kelly, _____ . She doesn't like parties!

Me: Were you dancing at 11:00?

Donna: No, I **9** _____ . I _____ on the phone.

Me: **10** Who _____ to?

Donna: My dad. I asked him to come and take us home.

Me: **11** What _____ at midnight?

Donna: I **12** _____ !

Vocabulary: The weather

4 ★ **Write questions about the weather in different cities and complete the answers.**

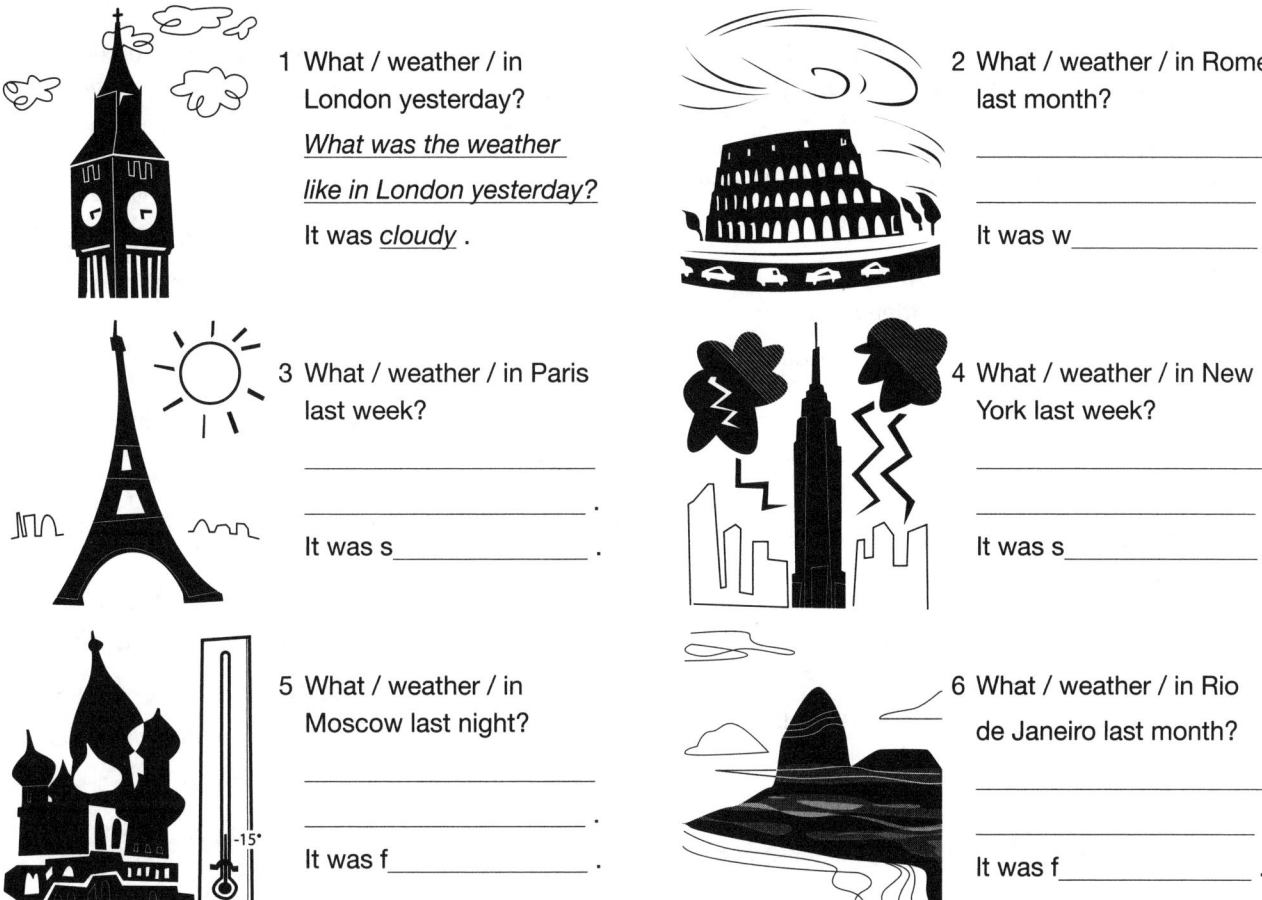

1 What / weather / in London yesterday?

What was the weather like in London yesterday?
It was *cloudy* .

2 What / weather / in Rome last month?

_____
_____ .
It was w_____ .

3 What / weather / in Paris last week?

_____
_____ .
It was s_____ .

4 What / weather / in New York last week?

_____
_____ .
It was s_____ .

5 What / weather / in Moscow last night?

_____
_____ .
It was f_____ .

6 What / weather / in Rio de Janeiro last month?

_____
_____ .
It was f_____ .

Consolidation

5 **Complete the conversation using the past continuous of the verbs in parentheses.**

Max: Hi, Laura. What **1** *were you doing* (you / do) yesterday afternoon? I tried to chat, but you didn't reply. **2** _____ (you / play) tennis?

Laura: No, I **3** _____ (not play) tennis. It **4** _____ (rain) all afternoon.

Max: Really? The sun **5** _____ (shine) here.

Laura: Well, it **6** _____ (not shine) here! I didn't turn on my computer because I **7** _____ (watch) TV. There was a great movie on. Did you see it?

Max: No. I **8** _____ (help) my parents. They **9** _____ (clean) the house for a party.

Laura: My dad **10** _____ (clean) the house, too.

Max: **11** _____ (he / get) ready for a party?

Laura: No, we're going to sell the house. We're going to move to Canada.

Max: Are you serious? When? You can't . . .

Laura: Ha ha! April Fool!

He was driving when . . .

Grammar: Past continuous and simple past with *while* and *when*

1 ★ Combine the parts of the sentences using *when*. Use the past continuous and simple past correctly.

Past continuous	Simple past
1 I watch TV	my friend call

I was watching TV when my friend called.

2 We lie on the beach it start rain

_____

_____

3 The burglar climb the ladder the police see him

_____

_____

4 You ride your bike you meet your friends

_____

_____

5 My dad drive home a police officer stop him

_____

_____

6 My mom jog she fall down

_____

_____

2 ★ Rewrite the sentences in Exercise 1 using *while*.

1 While I *was watching TV, my friend called* .

2 While we _____

_____ .

3 While the _____

_____ .

4 While you _____

_____ .

5 While my _____

_____ .

6 While my _____

_____ .

3 ★★ Complete the story with the correct form of the verbs in parentheses and *while* or *when*.

I 1 *was walking* (walk) into town last Saturday
2 w*hen* I *saw* (see) a strange man next to a car.
He 3 _____ (try) to open the car door.
4 W_____ I _____ (look) again, he
5 _____ (stand) by a different car!
This time, the door was open and he was looking
inside. 6 W_____ he _____ (do) this,
a police car 7 _____ (arrive).
The man 8 _____ (not see) it.
The police officers 9 _____ (get) out of their
car, but 10 w_____ they _____ (walk)
towards him, he suddenly 11 _____ (jump)
into the car and 12 _____ (drive) away. I didn't
see them again and forgot all about it.
Later, I 13 _____ (watch) TV
14 w_____ I _____ (see) the man. He
15 _____ (sit) in the back of a police car.
He wasn't very happy. The police officers
16 _____ (take) him to the police station in
their car.

Vocabulary: Prepositions of location and motion

4 ★ Complete the article. Use prepositions.

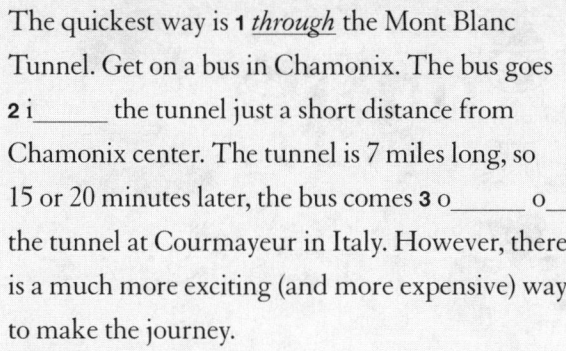

Crossing from Chamonix to Italy

There are two main ways to get from Chamonix in France to Italy.

The quickest way is **1** *through* the Mont Blanc Tunnel. Get on a bus in Chamonix. The bus goes **2** i_____ the tunnel just a short distance from Chamonix center. The tunnel is 7 miles long, so 15 or 20 minutes later, the bus comes **3** o_____ o__ the tunnel at Courmayeur in Italy. However, there is a much more exciting (and more expensive) way to make the journey.

You can go **4** o_____ the mountains in a special mountain car. You get on at Chamonix and go **5** u_____ to an amazing 13,123 feet (about 4,000 meters) at the Aiguille du Midi. A second car then takes you back **6** d_____ on the Italian side to La Palud.

Both Courmayeur and La Palud are just a two-hour bus ride from the beautiful town of Aosta, where you can drink Italian cappuccino and relax after your journey.

Consolidation

5 Look at the picture and read the paragraph. In your notebook, rewrite the underlined words or phrases to make the text correct. Start like this:

It was Saturday morning. I was going into a store . . .

It was Saturday morning. I was <u>coming out of</u> a store. <u>In</u> the store, there was a ladder. Melissa was standing <u>under</u> the ladder. Sean was walking <u>through a tunnel under</u> the road. Mrs. Tomkins was walking across <u>a bridge</u>. Mr. Davies was <u>riding a bike</u>. He was <u>riding a bike over</u> the bridge.

Extra challenge!

6 ★★★ Complete the paragraphs with words from the boxes.

Famous sporting events

What were you doing when the Indianapolis Colts won the 2010 Super Bowl?

> • find • not have • walk • watch • ~~when~~ • win

1 *When* the Colts **2** _____ the Super Bowl, I **3** _____ in the mountains with my friends. We **4** _____ a TV, but we **5** _____ a coffee shop with a TV. Lots of people **6** _____ the game. It was a great night.

What were you doing when the tennis player Roger Federer won his fifth Wimbledon?

> • leave • not do • not see • sit • when • work

I **7** _____ as a waitress in a coffee shop and, I **8** _____ any tennis that day. I remember, my brother **9** _____ anything that weekend. When I **10** _____ for work, he **11** _____ on the sofa, and he was still there **12** _____ I got home. He didn't even record it for me!

A monster that comes alive

Vocabulary: Types of movies

1 ★ Use the pictures for clues. Then write the types of movies. Finally, use the shaded boxes to discover the movie in the photo.

1	c	r	i	m	e			
2			t			n		
3			p					
4		n		a		e		
5		s	t					
6				m		d		
7	c			o				
8			r	r		r		
9		n		s				
10	r		m			c		
11	u		i		a			
12		r		l		r		

Grammar: Adjective clauses with *who*, *that*, and *where*

2 ★ Circle the correct words. Then match the movies from the box to the correct sentences about them.

> • *Avatar* • *Jurassic Park* • *King Kong* • *Madagascar* • *Shrek* • *The Bourne Supremacy*
> • *The Matrix* • *Titanic*

1 It's the place *who* / (*where*) Neo really lives. _____ *The Matrix* _____

2 They go to an island *where* / *that* there are dinosaurs. _____

3 It's about a ship *who* / *that* hits an iceberg. _____

4 The hero is a man *who* / *that* is running away from the CIA. _____

5 There's a giant gorilla *where* / *that* climbs the Empire State Building. _____

6 There are blue people *where* / *that* live on a faraway planet. _____

7 It's a country *who* / *where* some New York zoo animals go to. _____

8 It's about an ogre *where* / *that* has two friends—a donkey and a cat. _____

3 ★★ **Combine the two sentences using adjective clauses.**

1 This is Ben Stiller. He is in *Night at the Museum*.

This is Ben Stiller, who is in "Night at the Museum."

2 He goes to the New York Museum of Natural History. He gets a job there.

_____

_____

3 There are three old men. They work in the museum.

_____

_____

4 They give Ben some instructions. These tell him what to do at night.

_____

_____

5 There are lots of displays in the museum. They all come to life at night.

_____

_____

6 There is something magic in the museum. The old men want to steal it.

_____

_____

7 Ben makes friends with people. They help him stop the criminals.

_____

_____

Use your English: Buy tickets at the theater

4 ★ **Number the sentences in conversation order.**

	Mr. Dan:	Here you are.
	Mr. Dan:	How much is that?
	Mr. Dan:	The six o'clock movie.
	Mr. Dan:	Two adults and two children, please.
1	Mr. Dan:	Four tickets for *Iron Man 2*, please.
2	Clerk:	Adult or child?
	Clerk:	Thank you. Enjoy the movie.
	Clerk:	OK, and which showing?
	Clerk:	That's $40 all together.
	Clerk:	That's four for the six o'clock.

Consolidation

5 **Complete the conversation with the words from the box.**

> • action • animated • cartoons • ~~kind~~
> • romance • that • that • tickets • where
> • who • who

Lisa: What **1** *kind* of movie is *The Twilight Saga: Eclipse*?

Woman: It's about a girl **2** _____ loves a vampire, so it's a **3** _____ . But it's also a horror movie.

Lisa: Oh. I don't like movies **4** _____ are scary. What other movies are on?

Woman: Well, there's *Toy Story 3*. It's an **5** _____ film from Disney.

Lisa: That's about toys, right?

Woman: Yes. The toys are in a children's school, **6** _____ they have a lot of adventures.

Lisa: Hmm. . . . No, I don't like **7** _____ .

Woman: There's another movie **8** _____ is very exciting. It's called *The A-Team*. It's an **9** _____ movie. It's about a team of men **10** _____ used to be soldiers. Someone says they are criminals, and they try to show they aren't.

Lisa: OK. Two **11** _____ , please!

The history test

Before you read

1 Before you read, check the meaning of these words.

> **New words**
> • alone • break time • fights (*n*) • lie (*v*) • schoolyard • silent • surprised • turn red

Read

2 ★ Read the text. Fill in the blanks (1–5) with the sentences (a–e).

a) Josh sat there, silent.

b) The police often went there to stop fights.

c) ~~It was a normal day, and they were talking about football.~~

d) He didn't want to start now.

e) Josh was surprised.

Josh's problem

It was break time. Josh was standing in the schoolyard with his friends.
1 _c_ As the conversation stopped, Josh started talking about the history test in the next class. "I'm a little worried about the test," he said. "Did you study much for it?"

His friends smiled. "No, we didn't," replied Mark. "We didn't study at all."

2 ____ "But how are you going to pass the test?" Mark looked at Harry. "We aren't going to class. We're going to the Biker's Café." Josh knew the café. **3** ____ He tried to stop his friends, but the bell rang. He walked to the classroom alone.

While he was getting ready for the test, the teacher, Mr. Clarke, looked around the room. "Where are the others?" he asked. **4** ____ Mr. Clarke turned to him. "Josh, you're friends with Mark and Harry. Do you know where they are?" Josh's face turned red. He never lied. **5** ____ "Yes," he said, "I do."

3 ★★ **Read the story again and match the beginnings of the sentences (1–5) to the endings (a–e).**

1 Josh was a boy who _b_

2 Mr. Clarke was a teacher who ___

3 Mark was a boy who ___

4 The Biker's Café was a place where ___

5 The schoolyard was the place where ___

a) went to the café with Harry.

b) never lied.

c) there were often fights.

d) Josh and his friends went at break time.

e) taught history.

Listen

Listening tip: Focus your listening

Remember! Before you listen, read the questions carefully. Then listen for that information.

4 ★ **Knowing these questions and the kind of information to listen for will help you better understand the listening passage. Match the questions (1–8) to the information (a–h).**

1 Who did the school call? _b_

2 What can't Mark do for two weeks? ___

3 What can't Mark use for one week? ___

4 When is Mark going to take the history test? ___

5 What was the café like? ___

6 How old were the people there? ___

7 How long did the test last? ___

8 What did they watch after the test? ___

a) a thing

b) a person

c) an age

d) an activity

e) a length of time

f) a kind of movie

g) a day or date

h) an adjective

5 ★★ (7) **Now listen and answer the questions in Exercise 4.**

1 The school called _Mark's mom_ .

2 Mark can't _____ for two weeks.

3 Mark can't _____ for one week.

4 Mark is going to take the history test _____ _____ .

5 The café was _____ .

6 The people in the café were about _____ _____ .

7 The test lasted _____ .

8 After the test, they watched a _____ _____ about the 18th century.

Write

6 ★ **Think about what happened to Josh's other friend, Harry. On a piece of paper, complete the description.**

When the school called Harry, _____ answered the phone. He / She went to the school and asked Mr. Clarke about Harry: " . . ."

Mr. Clarke said: "Harry . . ."

When Harry's _____ got home, Harry _____ in his room. He went downstairs. His mother / father said: ". . ."

Harry went back to his room. He was very . . .

Vocabulary: Places in town

1 ★ Complete the places.

If you want to . . .	. . . you go to a(n):
1 get a room for the night	h _o_ _t_ _e_ _l_
2 see paintings	a _ _ g _ _ _ _ _ _
3 get better	h _ _ _ _ _ _ _
4 borrow books	l _ _ _ _ _ _
5 go to lots of stores	s _ _ _ _ _ _ _ m _ _ _
6 see a play	t _ _ _ _ _ _
7 buy a stamp	p _ _ _ o _ _ _ _ _
8 see interesting old things	m _ _ _ _ _

2 ★★ Complete the text with the words from the box.

- ~~gas~~ • hall • information • market • office
- police • ~~station~~ • station • tourist • town
- zoo

When we arrived in Oaxaca, it was dark and we couldn't find our hotel. Our map was outdated. When we stopped for gas at a **1** _gas station_ , we saw a police officer. He was very friendly and he took us to the **2** _____ _____ . People thought we were criminals when we went inside with him! He showed us a map, and we finally arrived at our hotel at 10 P.M. It was very nice, but noisy because of the birds in the **3** _____ next door!

The next day, we went to the **4** _____ _____ _____ to get some maps and information about Oaxaca. It was near the **5** _____ _____ , which was a beautiful building in the center of the city square. On the other side of the square, there was a big **6** _____ where people sold food and paintings.

Grammar: *too* + adjective (+ infinitive); *not* + adjective + *enough* (+ infinitive)

3 ★ Complete the sentences with *too* and the adjectives that describe life in big cities and villages.

Where is the best place to buy a new house?

Problems!

Big city
1 city – big
2 streets – crowded
3 buses – slow
4 air – dirty
5 downtown at night – dangerous

Village
6 village – small
7 weekends – quiet
8 nights – boring
9 village – far from my work
10 taxis to the city – expensive

1 The city _is too big_ .
2 The streets in the city _are too crowded_ .
3 The buses in the city _____

_____ .
4 The air in the city _____

_____ .
5 The downtown _____ at night.
6 The village _____ .
7 Weekends in the village _____

_____ .
8 Nights in the village _____

_____ .
9 The village _____ .
10 Taxis to the city _____

_____ .

4 ★★ Look at the pictures. Write sentences using the adjectives in parentheses.

1 "I can't sleep on this."

(tall) *I'm too tall.*

(big) *It's not big enough.*

2 "I can't eat that."

(hungry) _____

(big) _____

3 "I can't buy that."

(expensive) _____

(rich) _____

4 "I can't do this."

(smart) _____

(difficult) _____

5 "I can't use this."

(old) _____

(modern) _____

Consolidation

5 Write sentences using the correct form of *too* or *enough*.

Are you a Todd or a Taylor?

In the reality TV series *Always Greener*, two families, the Todds and the Taylors, change homes. The Taylors move to the Todds' farm, and the Todds move to the Taylors' house in the big city.

Liz and John Taylor with Sandra Todd

The Todds love their farm.

1 It's not very exciting, but (it / exciting / for them) *it's exciting enough for them* .

2 The nearest town isn't very big, but (it / big / for them) _____ .

The Taylors don't like it at all at first.

3 (It / not / interesting / for them) _____

_____

4 (It / quiet / for them) _____

5 (It / boring / for them) _____

The big city is also a strange place for the Todd family.

6 (It / big / for them) _____

7 (It / noisy / for them) _____

8 (It / not / relaxing / for them) _____

_____

9 (It / crowded / for them) _____

_____

10 (It / not / safe / for them) _____

Phrases

1 ★ Complete the conversations with the correct phrases from the box.

- a little old for you • come on • I can't wait
- it's my treat • remind me

1 Dan: Let me pay for the meal.

Steve: No, no. *It's my treat*.

2 Helen: Our summer vacation starts tomorrow!

Eva: _____ !

3 Paul: I'm worried about this test. I'm going to
fail, I'm sure.

Nick: _____ ! You always get the best grades.

4 Cathy: I love George Clooney!

Laura: Isn't he about 50?

He's _____ !

Cathy: Well, you like Brad Pitt, and he's only two
years younger.

5 Josh: Are you ready for today?

Phil: _____ . . . what are we doing?

Josh: We're going hiking in the mountains.

Phil: Oh, yes. I remember.

Grammar: Present continuous for future plans

2 ★ Look at Hannah's diary. Complete the text.

Monday:	see doctor 9 A.M.
Tuesday:	sing in concert 8 P.M.
Wednesday:	play for school basketball team 4 P.M.
Thursday:	meet Maria at the airport 3 P.M.; Maria here for one week
Friday:	have party for Maria – 8 P.M.
Saturday:	Maria and I go to Portland (take 8 A.M. train); stay one night – with my uncle and aunt.
Sunday:	home – get 11 A.M. train; visit Sue and Rob 7 P.M.
Monday:	Maria – takes English test 9 A.M.

It's going to be a busy week. **1** *I'm seeing* the doctor
on Monday morning (nothing serious!). On Tuesday
night, **2** _____ in a concert. I hope
I'm OK! On Wednesday, **3** _____
basketball for the school team—my first game!
I hope Ben comes to watch me! Then on Thursday,
4 _____ Maria at the airport. On
Friday, my parents and I **5** _____ a party for
Maria at our house. Then on Saturday, Maria and
I **6** _____ to Portland. **7** _____
the eight o'clock train and we **8** _____ for
one night with my uncle and aunt at their house in
Portland. (They're meeting us at the train station.) On
Sunday morning, **9** _____ the eleven o'clock
train home, and that night **10** _____
Sue and Rob. On Monday, Maria **11** _____ an
English test. I hope she passes. Then she can come
back in September for a whole year!

**3 ★★ Write questions using the cues. Find the
answers in Exercise 2.**

1 What / Hannah / do on Monday?

What's Hannah doing on Monday?

She's seeing the doctor at nine o'clock.

2 she / do / anything on Tuesday morning?

_____

_____

3 When / she / play / basketball?

_____

_____

4 Where / she / meet Maria?

_____

_____

5 What / Maria and Hannah / do on Saturday?

_____

_____

6 What time / they / come / back?

_____

_____

Vocabulary: Transportation

4 ★ **Rearrange the letters to make forms of transportation.**

Two wheels

1 c e y o r o t m l c   *motorcycle*

2 o m d p e   _____

In the air

3 n a l e p   _____

4 l p e t h i c e r o   _____

On water

5 r y f e r   _____

6 p h i s   _____

On rails

7 n i a r t   _____

8 y s b u a w   _____

Four wheels

9 n v a   _____

You can go camping in it

10 a r t i e r l   _____

Consolidation

5 **Complete the conversation with the correct words or form of the words from the box.**

> • are • by • come • for • get • go • stay
> • too • trailer • wait

Matt: **1** *Are* you going on vacation this year?

Joe: Yes, I am. I can't **2** _____ ! I'm going to the mountains.

Matt: Who are you **3** _____ with?

Joe: I'm going with Adam and Becky.

Matt: Becky's a little old **4** _____ you!

Joe: Ha, ha! Very funny! She's one year older than me, and she's just a friend.

Matt: How are you **5** _____ there?

Joe: We're going **6** _____ train.

Matt: Are you **7** _____ in a hotel?

Joe: **8** _____ on! Hotels are **9** _____ expensive for us. We're staying in a **10** _____ . It's small, but it's very cheap.

Matt: Does it have a roof?

Joe: Oh, yes. Well, I hope so. . . .

Extra challenge!

6 ★★★ **Follow the lines and complete the sentences about the people.**

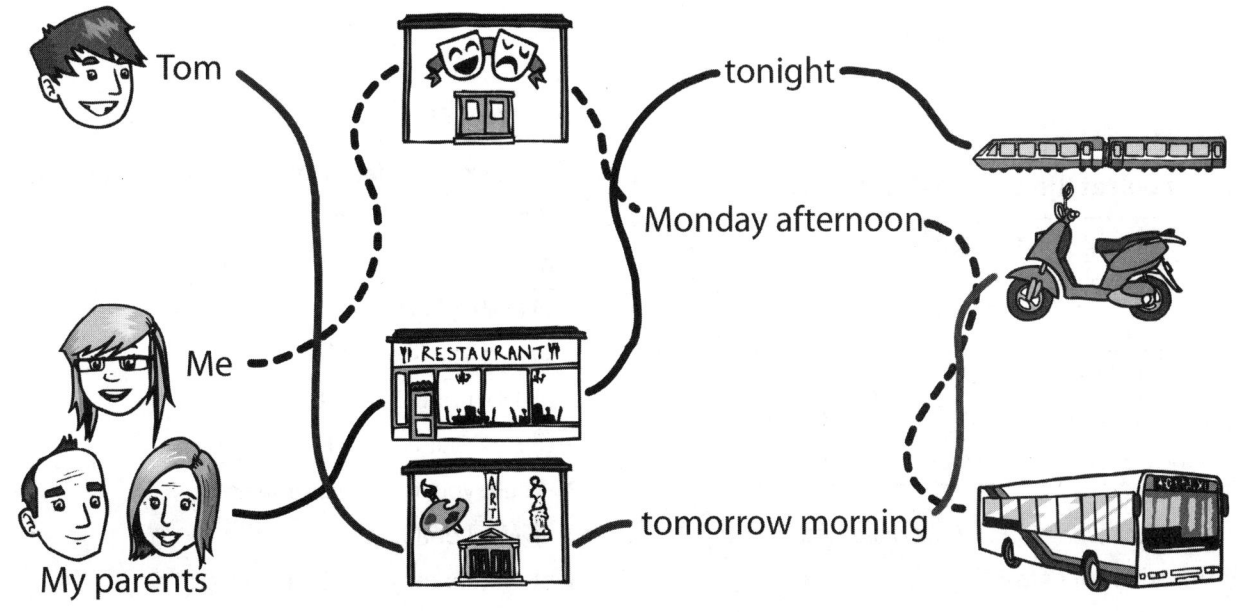

1 Tom *is going to an art gallery tomorrow morning* .

   He*'s going by moped* .

2 I _____ .

  I _____ .

3 My parents _____

_____ .

  They _____

_____ .

I'd like lasagna, please.

Vocabulary: Restaurant food

1 ★ Match the words (1–12) to words (a–l).

Meat

| 1 roast | _c_ | a) soup |
| 2 steak | ____ | b) salad |

Fish

| 3 baked, | ____ | c) beef |
| 4 fish | ____ | d) ice cream |

Pasta

| 5 spaghetti | ____ | e) coffee |

Side orders

6 mashed	____	f) pie
7 garlic	____	g) water
8 green	____	h) bolognese

Desserts

| 9 apple | ____ | i) stuffed salmon |
| 10 vanilla | ____ | j) tartare |

Drinks

| 11 bottled | ____ | k) potatoes |
| 12 decaffeinated | ____ | l) bread |

Grammar: *like*

2 ★ Look at the chart and write sentences.

	Mel and Kim	**Me**	**Phil**
Steak	✓	✗	✗
Grilled fish	✗	✓	✓
Garlic prawns	✓	✗	✗
Lasagna	✗	✗	✓
Cheesecake	✓	✓	✓

1 I / grilled fish _____I like grilled fish._____

2 Mel and Kim / steak _____

3 I / garlic prawns _____

4 Phil / steak _____

5 Phil / cheesecake _____

6 Mel and Kim / lasagna _____

3 ★★ Write questions and short answers about the information in Exercise 2.

1 Phil / grilled fish?

   Does Phil like grilled fish?

   Yes, he does.

2 you / steak?

   _____

   _____

3 Mel and Kim / grilled fish?

   _____

   _____

4 Phil / lasagna?

   _____

   _____

5 Mel and Kim / cheesecake?

   _____

   _____

6 Phil / garlic prawns?

   _____

   _____

Grammar: *like* and *would like*

4 ★ Circle the letter of the correct response.

1 What do you like for dinner?

   a) I'll have roast chicken, please.

   b) Fish, chicken . . . sometimes vegetarian food.

2 Would you like beef?

   a) No, not today, thank you.

   b) Yes, but I'm not hungry today.

3 Would you like garlic prawns?

   a) No, I don't.

   b) No, thank you. I don't like garlic.

4 I like spaghetti . . .

   a) and I often eat it.

   b) today, please.

Use your English: Order food in a restaurant

5 ★ Complete the conversation (1–6) with the questions (a–f).

a) What would you like to drink?
b) Would you like some garlic bread with that?
c) Are you ready to order?
d) Can we have the check, please?
e) What would you like?
f) Anything else?

Waitress: 1 _c_

James: Yes, we are.

Waitress: 2 _____

James: Something special. Special, but inexpensive! We'd like three lasagnas, please.

Waitress: 3 _____

James: Oh, yes, please. That would be great. I love garlic.

Waitress: 4 _____

James: We'll have three sodas, please.

Waitress: 5 _____

James: Not for me, thanks.

Hannah: Could I have a salad, please?

Luke: Can I have one, too?

James: Oh, right. Sorry. Two salads, please.

***

James: 6 _____

Waitress: Of course. Here you are.

Hannah: How much is it?

James: Eighteen dollars. That's six dollars each.

Consolidation

6 Complete the online chat with the words from the box. Use the correct form for the verbs.

• bread • to go • ~~like~~ • like • like • like
• not like • not like • not like • tartare

Vicky: Hi, Noemi. ☹

Noemi: Hi, Vicky. Are you OK?

Vicky: Not really. I'm going out to eat with my parents tonight. I **1** _'d like_ to stay at home, but I can't.

Noemi: Why? I love going out to restaurants!

Vicky: I **2** _____ going out to restaurants— well, just not with my parents! Dad **3** _____ steak that's red in the center. Mom always eats steak **4** _____ !

Noemi: What's that?

Vicky: It's steak that isn't cooked!

Noemi: Yuck!

Vicky: They also **5** _____ garlic—garlic **6** _____ , garlic prawns.

Noemi: Garlic's good. I always cook with garlic.

Vicky: I'd like **7** _____ to a vegetarian restaurant, but my dad **8** _____ vegetarian food. I don't know why he's taking me tonight. He **9** _____ taking me out.

Noemi: Yes, he does. He took us to a Chinese restaurant last month for your birthday. Remember? That was great. I **10** _____ to eat there again, but it's too expensive for me. Do you know where you're going tonight?

Vicky: I think it's a French restaurant.

Noemi: OK. See you tomorrow, and bon appétit! ☺

Across cultures

Takeout restaurants

Before you read

1 Before you read, check the meaning of these words.

> **New words**
> • batter (*n*) • chili (pepper) • curry • fry
> • sundae • takeout

Read

2 ★ Read the texts and match words (1–6) with words (a–f).

1 Sonic	*b*	a)	chips
2 fast	____	b)	Drive-In
3 fish and	____	c)	peas
4 mushy	____	d)	restaurant
5 pea	____	e)	soup
6 takeout	____	f)	food

3 ★★ Read the article again. Correct the mistakes in the sentences.

not popular
1 Sonic Drive-In restaurants are ~~popular~~ in the U.K.

2 The Coney is a hamburger with chilies and cheese.

3 Simon loves the Candy Sundae.

4 Michelle tried curry and chips at an Indian restaurant in Vancouver, Canada.

5 Michelle doesn't like curry.

Sonic Drive-Ins and fish and chips!

Simon

We know a lot of American fast-food restaurants because there are a lot here in the U.K. But Sonic Drive-In® restaurants were new for me. In some ways, Sonic Drive-Ins are like McDonald's® or Burger King.® I mean, it's fast food. But the menu is amazing. I loved the Coneys—that's a hot dog with chilis and cheese on it. It's hot! And they do awesome drinks. The Lemon Slush is my favorite. I don't know why we don't have Sonics over here. One thing I didn't like was the Candy Sundae. I tried one, but it was awful. It was too sweet!

Michelle

When I came to the U.K. to visit, I had heard about fish and chips, or french fries. I sometimes go to Vancouver in Canada—it isn't far from my home in the U.S.—and they have restaurants from the U.K. there. But there were still some strange things that I hadn't tried yet so I tried fish and chips. The fish is in batter and is fried. I also had mushy peas. They're like pea soup—they look disgusting, but they actually taste pretty good. There was one thing I didn't like. I went to an Indian takeout restaurant. My U.K. friends had curry and chips, not curry and rice. I tried curry and chips and really didn't like it! I mean, I like curry and I like chips, but not together!

Listen

4 ★ 🎧 **8** **Listen and complete the sentences.**

1 The name of the waitress is _Candy_ .

2 Brad orders two _____ to drink.

3 Jack doesn't understand everything on the _____ .

4 A Texas steak weighs about _____ .

5 They decide to have Mexican _____ and _____ .

6 They have tortilla chips with two _____ to start.

7 Jack loves the _____ in the U.S.

Write

> **Writing tip: Conjunctions: _both . . . and,_ _either . . . or_**
>
> **Remember!** We can join two things in one sentence by using pairs of conjunctions, for example, _both . . . and, either . . . or._
> _Italian and Chinese restaurants are popular in_ **both** _London_ **and** _New York._
> _People go to_ **either** _burger_ **or** _pizza restaurants._

5 ★ **Use the conjunctions from the tip box to complete the sentences so that they mean the same as the first ones.**

1 There are a lot of Italian restaurants in New York. There are a lot of Italian restaurants in Chicago.

There are lots of Italian restaurants in _both_ New York _and_ Chicago.

2 Is pizza popular? Is curry popular? Are _____ pizza _____ curry?

3 We can eat in a Chinese restaurant. We can eat in an Indian restaurant.

We can eat _____ in a Chinese restaurant _____ in an Indian restaurant.

4 I'd like a steak. I'd like a hamburger, too. I'm hungry!

I'd like _____ a steak _____ a hamburger.

5 We can go to a restaurant. We can get takeout.

We can _____ .

6 Do your grandparents eat meat? Do your parents eat meat?

_____

eat meat?

7 La Hacienda is a good restaurant. Pasta Palace is a good restaurant.

_____

_____ good restaurants.

6 ★★ **Look at the information about two different restaurants. On a piece of paper, write an e-mail to a friend to help him or her decide where to eat.**

Pasta and Pasta (P+P)	**Chez Noo**
Good food ✓	Good food ✓
Big portions ✓	Big portions ✓
Cheap ✗	Cheap ✗
Italian and Greek food	French and Chinese food

From: Magali
To: Julio

Hi Julio,
Where are we going to eat? There are two places I know: Pasta and Pasta and Chez Noo. Both P+P and Chez Noo serve good food.
Both . . .
Both . . .
At P+P you can eat either . . .
At Chez Noo . . .
Let me know what you think.
Magali

Which one do you like?

Phrases/Use your English

1 ★ Complete the conversations with the phrases from the box.

• How does it look • It's more my style • It's too ugly • They don't look right

1 **Terry:** I don't like these jeans.

   Paul: Why not?

   Terry: I don't know. *They don't look right* .

2 **Rachel:** Do you want to try this skirt on?

   Danielle: No, I like this one. _____ .

3 **Carly:** _____ ?

   Denise: Hmm. It's OK, but I prefer shirts with patterns.

4 **Jerry:** Hey! Look at this hat. Try it on.

   Lesley: No! _____ !

Vocabulary: Clothes, accessories, and styles

2 ★ Complete the words.

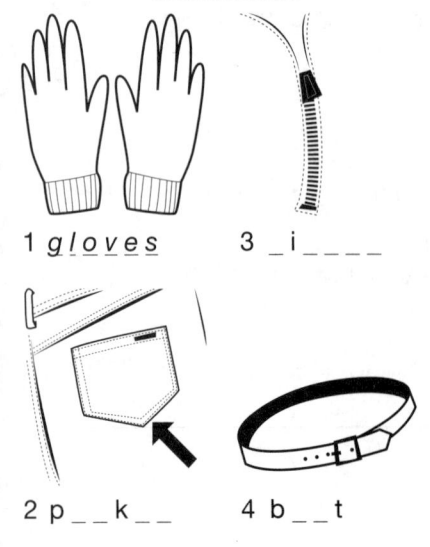

accessories

1 *gloves*

3 _i _ _ _ _

2 p _ _ k _ _

4 b _ t

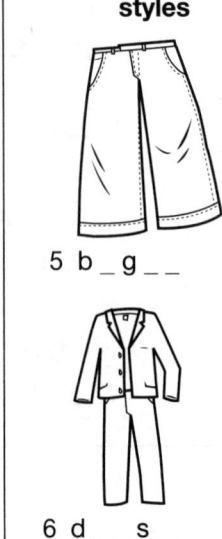

styles

5 b _ g _ _

6 d _ _ s _ _

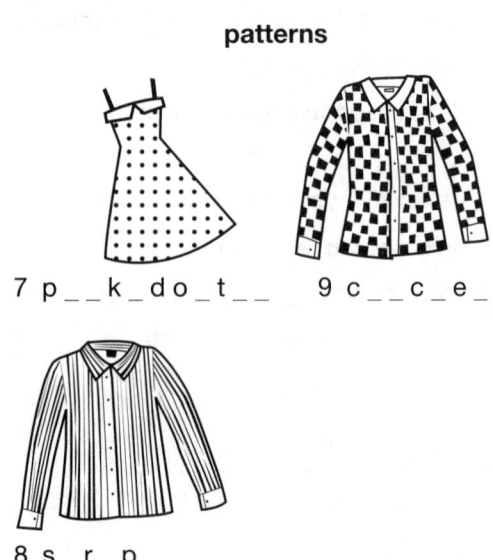

patterns

7 p _ _ k _ d o _ t _ _

9 c _ _ c e _

8 s _ r _ p _ _

Grammar: Indefinite pronoun *one/ones*

3 ★ **Complete the conversations with *one* or *ones*.**

A

Mark: Which shirt should I buy? The striped
1 *one* or the plain **2** _____ ?

Josh: Which **3** _____ do you prefer?

Mark: Well, usually I prefer plain **4** _____ , but
I don't know.

Josh: Well, try the striped **5** _____ on and see
what it looks like.

B

Nick: Do you like these jeans?

Ana: Which **6** _____ ?

Nick: The blue **7** _____ .

Ana: What, those baggy **8** _____ ?

Nick: No, the **9** _____ with zippers on the
pockets. Ask one of those sales clerks
if you can try them on.

Ana: OK. Which **10** _____ ? The girl with
blond hair over there?

4 ★★ **Number the sentences in the
conversation in the correct order.**

1	a) **Malcolm:**	I don't know what to wear to the party.
	b) **Joe:**	Oh, I see. So wear a striped shirt. It would look good.
	c) **Malcolm:**	Which one?
	d) **Joe:**	Wear a T-shirt.
	e) **Joe:**	Your old baggy one.
	f) **Malcolm:**	That T-shirt isn't very dressy. I want to look good.
	g) **Joe:**	You don't? They have some at Top Store. They're only $10.
	h) **Malcolm:**	I don't have a striped shirt.
9	i) **Malcolm:**	Really? Let's go there now! We can take the bus.

Use your English: Choosing clothes to wear

5 ★ **Complete the text with the words from the box.**

• like • look • look • prefer • should • ~~think~~ • too
• too • wear

Hey, guys. It's Laura's party on Friday. I have these new clothes. What do you **1** *think*? Do you **2** _____ them? Send me some comments—please!

• I don't like those pants. They're **3** _____ short. *Julia*

• I don't agree with Julia. I think they
4 _____ good. You **5** _____ good.
See you at the party. *Sara*

• I love the pants, but the shirt is
6 _____ flowery. *Luz*

• I think so, too. Why don't you **7** _____
something plainer? *Sergio*

• I **8** _____ skirts to pants. But, hey,
you look good in anything. *Maria*

• You had a great dress last year. You
9 _____ wear it again this year! *Ana*

Consolidation

6 **Rearrange the letters into words to complete the sentences.**

1 My (gygba) *baggy* jeans don't (kolo) _____ good on me,
and my (gttih) _____ jeans are (oot) _____ small.

2 This (trspide) _____ shirt is (oto) _____ big. The
(ilapn) _____ one isn't my (eyslt) _____ .

3 I don't (olok) _____ good in (uaclsa) _____ clothes,
but I (rrepfe) _____ them to (yrdess) _____ clothes.

4 What (lhsuod) _____ I wear? What do you (hitkn) _____ ?
The blue shirt or the red shirt? (ihhcw) _____ one?

5 I want a (kdcehec) _____ shirt with a (ktopec)
_____ on the front, but I can't find (neo) _____ .

8B If my friend has a problem . . .

Vocabulary: Personality adjectives

1 ★ Write the negative adjectives under Nick's picture. Write the positive adjectives under Penny's picture.

1 neat / messy	5 cheap / generous
2 bossy / helpful	6 friendly / unfriendly
3 lazy / hard-working	7 bad-tempered / easy-going
4 polite / rude	8 funny / annoying

Nick

1 _messy_ _____
2 _____
3 _____
4 _____
5 _____
6 _____
7 _____
8 _____

Penny

1 _neat_ _____
2 _____
3 _____
4 _____
5 _____
6 _____
7 _____
8 _____

2 ★★ Complete the personality adjectives to describe these people.

1 Chris is very s_mart_. He always does well on tests.
2 Henrietta is very h_____-w_____ . She always does lots of work.
3 Tim is very n_____ . Everything in his room is in the right place.
4 Sue is s_____ . She finds it hard to talk to people.
5 Quentin is very q_____ . Sometimes you don't know he is there.
6 Gina is very g_____ . She often gives presents to her friends.
7 Paul is very p_____ . He always says "Please" and "Thank you."
8 My brother is very b_____ . He always tells me what to do.
9 Laura is very l_____ . She never says bad things about her friends.
10 Alonzo is very h_____ . He never tells lies.

Grammar:
Conditional: *if* clause + present

3 ★ Complete the sentences with the correct form of the verbs in parentheses.

1 If I _have_ (have) a problem, my mom always _helps_ (help) me.
2 If my father _____ (go) to bed late, he _____ (be) bad-tempered in the morning.
3 If my sister _____ (play) her music too loudly, my mom _____ (shout) at her.
4 If my brother _____ (have) lots of homework, he _____ (eat) his dinner in his room.
5 If my brother _____ (not have) any homework, he _____ (practice) the guitar and _____ (write) songs.
6 If my sister _____ (get up) late, she _____ (not have) breakfast.
7 If there _____ (be) football on TV, my father always _____ (watch) it.
8 If we _____ (be) noisy, our teacher _____ (give) us lots of homework.

4 ★★ Use verbs from the box in the correct form to complete the sentences.

> • buy • do • get • have • hear • not look • play • ~~see~~ • turn • ~~want~~ • not wear • win

1 If I *see* her wearing nice
   clothes, I always *want* to
   buy them.

3 If she _____
   school work, she always
   _____ it well—just
   like Hermione!

5 If he _____ his
   glasses, he _____
   like Harry Potter.

2 If he _____ other
   sports, _____ he
   usually _____ ?

4 If someone _____
   a pixel on this website,
   Alex Tew _____ $1.

6 If you _____ their
   songs on the radio, _____
   you _____ it off?

Consolidation

5 Complete the sentences with the correct form of the verbs in parentheses and the correct personality adjectives from the box.

> • annoying • bad-tempered • easy-going
> • ~~funny~~ • honest • smart

1 If my friend *tells* (tell) us a story, we always *laugh*
   (laugh). She's very *funny*.

2 If we _____ (not be) quiet, our teacher
   _____ (shout) at us and _____
   (bang) on his desk. He's very _____ .

3 If my brother _____ (want) to borrow a
   CD, he just _____ (take) it without asking.
   He's very _____ .

4 If we _____ (have) a test, Tessa always
   _____ (do) well. She's very _____ .

5 If Ben _____ (find) something in the street,
   he _____ (not keep) it. He _____ (take)
   it to the police station. He's very _____ .

6 If there _____ (be) problems, my mom
   _____ (not worry) and she _____
   (not get) upset. She just _____ (smile) and
   _____ (say): "Don't worry!"
   She's very _____ .

Extra challenge!

6 ★★★ Read the text and match the people (1–6) to the personality adjectives (a–f) that describe them.

> a) shy   ~~c) unfriendly~~   e) cheap
> b) messy   d) bossy   f) lazy

1 If Lucy meets people she knows, she never
   says hello or smiles. She doesn't like people
   very much.   [c]

2 If Alex's teacher doesn't stand next to him, he
   doesn't do any work. He hates working.   [ ]

3 If Elena goes out to eat, she leaves a
   small tip.   [ ]

4 If Neil goes to a party and he doesn't know
   anyone, he doesn't talk. He stands alone.   [ ]

5 If Jacob is in a group, he always tells the others
   what to do. He does it in class, and he does it
   when he's playing sports.   [ ]

6 If Natasha's mother doesn't tell her to clean up,
   she never puts anything away.   [ ]

He's really cute.

Vocabulary: Physical appearance

1 ★ Complete the descriptions with one adjective of general appearance and one of build.

1 She's a b e_a_u_t_i_f_u l woman. She's tall and s l_i_m .

2 He's very h _ n _ _ o _ _ and w _ l _ b _ _ l _ .

3 They're o _ d _ n _ _ _- l _ _ k _ _ _ people. They're both of m _ d _ _ _ b _ _ l _ .

4 He's a very u _ l _ man. He's short and t _ i _ .

5 She's a very p _ _ t _ y girl. She's tall and h _ _ _ y .

6 They're g _ _ d- l _ _ k _ _ g boys, but they're l _ r _ _ .

Grammar: *be like* and *look like*

2 ★ Write questions for the answers using the cues in parentheses.

1 *What's your father like?* (your father)
He's hard-working and intelligent.

2 _____ (you)
I'm happy and easy-going.

3 _____ (Tom Cruise)
He's short and well built.

4 _____ (Adam Sandler and Chris Rock)
They're smart and funny.

5 _____ (Selena Gomez)
She's short and slim with long, black hair.

3 ★★ Write questions and answers. Use *be like* or *look like* in the questions and the words from the box in the answers.

> • black • handsome • intelligent • smile
> • tall

Boss: OK. We have an idea for a new TV show. It's about a family living in New York. Now, we need some actors. First, the father. Any ideas?

Assistant: What **1** *does* the character *look like* ?

Boss: A little strange. Not **2** *handsome* , but not ugly. Tall and thin.

Assistant: What about Ray Romano?

Boss: What **3** _____ he _____ ?

Assistant: He's **4** _____ . About 6 feet tall. He has short, **5** _____ hair. He's Italian-American and he's from New York.

Boss: I like it. What **6** _____ he _____ ?

Assistant: He's very **7** _____ and funny.

Boss: Call him now! Now, the girl. His daughter.

Assistant: I know: Megan Fox.

Boss: No, no. She can't be the daughter.

Assistant: Well, what **8** _____ the daughter _____ ?

Boss: She has a nice **9** _____ . That's important. Someone with a friendly face.

Assistant: I know: Demi Lovato.

Boss: What **10** _____ she _____ ?

Assistant: She's very cute and hard-working.

Boss: OK, great work. Let's have lunch and think about the rest of the children later.

Grammar: Adverbs: *pretty, a little, kind of, very, really* + adjective

4 ★ Write the words in parentheses in the correct order.

Dimitar Berbatov is a **1** <u>very good</u> (good / very) soccer player. He's one of the best soccer players in Europe today. Some people think he's **2** _____ (a little / lazy). Is it true? Berbatov says "No!" When he talks, he's always **3** _____ (honest / very). Dimitar says he's **4** _____ (hardworking / really) on the field, but he's also **5** _____ (intelligent / very) when he plays soccer. Some players are **6** _____ (kind of / silly). They run and run, but later they're too tired to play. Berbatov doesn't do that. He thinks that's a **7** _____ (really / unintelligent) thing to do. Berbatov isn't just a good soccer player. He's **8** _____ (handsome / very), too. He is one of Bulgaria's top-ten hottest men! Life is good for Berbatov right now. He is **9** _____ (happy / very) playing soccer.

Consolidation

5 Write questions and answers using the cues and then match them to the correct photo.

a David Archuleta   b Jonas Brothers   c Kanye West   d Brenda Song

1 | a | What / look ?
a friendly face (pretty) / cute (really)
<u>What does he look like?</u>
<u>He has a pretty friendly face and he's really cute.</u>

2 | | What / like ?
sometimes angry (kind of) / but / smart (really) / and / good at writing songs (very)
_____ ?
_____
_____

3 | | What / look ?
sweet (very) / has / black hair / Her eyes / big (pretty)
_____ ?
_____
_____

4 | | What / like ?
friendly (kind of) / and / nice (really) / good at singing (very)
_____ ?
_____
_____

Curriculum link: Science

INTEGRATED

CONSOLIDATION

SKILLS

Do opposites attract?

Before you read

1 Before you read, check the meaning of these words.

> **New words**
> • both • celebrity • get together • outgoing • to get along with someone

Personal and private lives

Sometimes people just get along very well, despite their differences. This week, we're looking at some people who are friends and stay friends. What **enables** some people to get along so well?

Ben Affleck and Matt Damon

Ben Affleck's family moved to Cambridge, Massachusetts, when he was eight. He soon became friends with a boy who was two years older than he was. His name was Matt Damon. Ben always wanted to be an actor. He started acting on TV when he was eight. Matt also liked acting, but he studied hard. He went to Harvard University to study English. They worked together and won an Oscar for the film *Good Will Hunting*. Ben was often in the newspapers because of his celebrity girlfriends, Jennifer Lopez and Gwyneth Paltrow. Matt also had girlfriends, but kept his **personal life** more **private**. They are both now married and want to work together again in the future.

Vanessa Hudgens and Ashley

The two Disney stars Vanessa Hudgens and Ashley Tisdale **have a lot in common.** They are both really pretty, and they can both act and sing well. But Vanessa and Ashley have their differences, too. Vanessa was born in California, and she is part Irish, Native American, Chinese, Filipino, and Spanish. Ashley is from New Jersey, and she is Jewish. Vanessa is kind of outgoing and **bold**. Ashley is more careful than Vanessa. She is sweet and funny. Vanessa and Ashley became good friends on the set of the *High School Musical* movies. They love to hang out together and shop. These days, the two friends spend a lot of time with their boyfriends. Vanessa is dating Zac Efron, and Ashley is dating Scott Speer. But they get together as much as they can. Last New Year's Eve, Ashley posted this on her Twitter account: "So excited for tonight, gonna be bringin in the new year with my man, nessa, and zac!!!"

Read

> **Learning strategy: Guess meaning from context**
>
> **Remember!** When you find a new word in a text, don't stop reading. Try to guess the meaning from the context.

2 ★ Read the article. Circle the letter for the best meaning (a or b) of the words in bold.

1 enables

   (a) makes it possible for

   b) makes it impossible for

2 personal life

   a) a person's work

   b) a person's family and relationships

3 private

   a) other people know about it

   b) only you know about it

4 have a lot in common

   a) be similar

   b) be very different

5 bold

   a) shy

   b) not shy

3 ★ Match the people (1–4) with the correct facts (a–d).

1 Matt Damon ___d___   a) is part Filipino.

2 Ben Affleck _____   b) is careful and sweet.

3 Vanessa Hudgens _____ c) dated Jennifer Lopez.

4 Ashley Tisdale _____   d) went to Harvard

                             University.

4 ★★ Read the article. Answer the questions.

1 How old was Ben Affleck when his family moved to Cambridge, Massachusetts?

   He was eight years old.

2 What did Ben Affleck always want to be?

   _____

3 What did Matt Damon study at Harvard University?

   _____

4 Why was Ben Affleck often in the newspapers?

   _____

5 What do Vanessa Hudgens and Ashley Tisdale have in common?

   _____

6 Why don't Vanessa and Ashley see each other very often these days?

   _____

Listen

5 ★ 🎧 9 Listen and complete the chart.

	Danny	Rebecca
Personality	1 *quiet* and 2 _____	3 _____ and 4 _____
Clothes	old, 5 _____ clothes	new, 6 _____ clothes
Likes	7 _____	8 _____
Favorite color	9 _____	10 _____

Write

6 ★ Write a description of two famous people you like who are pretty different from each other. Take notes below and then write a paragraph about them on a piece of paper.

	Person 1	Person 2
Name	_____	_____
Appearance		
General	_____	_____
Hair	_____	_____
Face	_____	_____
Build	_____	_____
Personality	_____	_____
	_____	_____
Interests	_____	_____

Have you ever . . .?

Vocabulary: Vacation activities

1 ★ Complete the words for the activities.

1 go _skiing_

2 s _ _ b _ t _ _

3 go c _ n _ _ i _ _

4 go r _ _ _
   c _ _ m _ _ g

5 go s _ r _ _ n

6 go m _ u _ _ a _ _
   b _ k _ _ _

7 go w _ _ d u _ _ i _

8 go s _ g _ _ s _ _ i _ _

9 go s _ o _ _ i _ _

10 go h _ _ s _ b _ c _
    r _ _ i _ _

Grammar: The definite article with places

2 ★ Rewrite the sentences using two articles correctly with names of places.

1 When I went to U.S., I climbed Rocky Mountains.
   When I went to the U.S., I climbed the Rocky
   Mountains.

2 We stayed in Canary Islands, in Atlantic Ocean near Africa.

   _____

   _____

3 Hawaiian Islands are in Pacific Ocean.

   _____

   _____

4 Is Gobi Desert in Asia or U.S.?

   _____

   _____

5 My friend went to Brazil, but he didn't see Amazon River, and he didn't swim in Atlantic Ocean.

   _____

   _____

Grammar: Present perfect with *ever* and *never*

3 ★ Find and circle eight more past participles in the word search. Then write them next to the infinitive forms of the verbs.

S	E	E	N	A	M	O
W	R	I	T	T	E	N
U	S	L	E	P	T	E
M	E	A	T	B	E	N
R	I	D	D	E	N	D
A	E	A	T	E	N	T
P	R	D	O	N	E	O

1 be   _been_
2 do   _____
3 eat   _____
4 meet _____
5 ride _____
6 see   _____
7 sleep _____
8 swim _____
9 write _____

4 ★ Complete the sentences with the present perfect form of the verbs in parentheses.

1 I *'ve been* (be) to Australia, but I *'ve never been* (never be) to the U.S.

2 My father _____ (see) the Taj Mahal, but he _____ (never see) the Pyramids.

3 My brother _____ (meet) a prince, but he _____ (never meet) a rock star.

4 My mother _____ (ride) a camel, but she _____ (never ride) a horse.

5 My friends _____ (eat) Chinese food, but they _____ (never eat) Japanese food.

6 My sister _____ (swim) with dolphins, but she _____ (never swim) with whales.

7 My uncle _____ (write) two books, but he _____ (never write) an e-mail.

8 My aunt _____ (sleep) on a beach, but she _____ (never sleep) in a hotel.

9 We _____ (do) lots of amazing things!

5 ★★ Complete the ad.

1 (you / ever / eat) *Have you ever eaten* real Italian pizza?

2 (you / ever / swim) _____ in an Olympic-sized swimming pool?

3 (you / ever / see) _____ Italy in the spring?

4 (you / ever / sleep) _____ in a wonderful, five-star hotel?

5 (you / ever / go) _____ shopping on the island of Murano?

6 (you / ever / ride) _____ in a gondola?

7 (you / ever / write) _____ postcards in a coffee shop on St. Mark's Square?

8 (you / ever / meet) _____ warm, friendly people in a warm, friendly city?

9 (you / ever / be) _____ to Venice?

If the answer is "no," come to see us this May for a long weekend at the magnificent Hotel San Marco in Venice, Italy. See our website for more details and prices.

Consolidation

6 Complete the conversations with the correct form of the words from the box.

| • buy • ~~ever~~ • have • have • go • never • not have • not have • play • the • they |

Nick: Have you **1** *ever* been skiing in **2** _____ Rocky Mountains?

Liz: No, I **3** _____ , but I've **4** _____ beach volleyball on Venice Beach in Los Angeles.

Sara: **5** _____ your mom ever **6** _____ to the Saks Fifth Avenue store in New York?

Kelly: No, she **7** _____ , but she's **8** _____ some clothes from the Saks Fifth Avenue store in Atlanta.

Alan: **9** _____ your friends ever watched whales?

Rob: Yes, **10** _____ have, but they've **11** _____ swum with them!

Have you put up your tent yet?

Phrases

1 ★ Write the phrases (a–d) in the correct order. Then use them to complete the conversations (1–4).

a) down calm   *Calm down* !

b) no I have idea   _____

c) the problem now what's _____ ?

d) you I one owe   _____ .

1 A: Help! Help! Look! A snake!

  B: *Calm down!*

2 A: Wait a minute. Stop!

  B: _____

  A: I've lost my camera. I think I left it in that store.

3 A: Could I borrow a dollar for a bag of chips?

  B: Sure, no problem. Here you are.

  A: Thanks. _____

4 A: Do you know how to write *England* in Spanish?

  B: No, sorry, _____ , but I do have a dictionary in my bag.

Grammar: Present perfect with *already* and *yet*

2 ★ Circle the correct words.

1 Teacher: Please do Exercise 6.

  Students: We've (already) / yet done that.

2 Student: Can I go to the bathroom?

  Teacher: Again? But you've *already / yet* been!

3 Students: How did we do on the test?

  Teacher: I haven't finished grading your tests *already / yet*.

4 Teacher: Where's your homework, Sean?

  Student: I haven't finished it *yet / already*.

5 Student: What page are we on?

  Teacher: I've *yet / already* told you five times today.

6 Student: When does class start?

  Teacher: It's *yet / already* started, Elena.

7 Teacher: When is your big soccer game, Mario?

  Student: I've *already / yet* played the big game!

8 Student 1: What's the answer to number three?

  Student 2: I don't know. I haven't finished number two *yet / already*.

3 ★★ Complete the article with the correct form of the verbs in parentheses and *already* or *yet*.

Local boys with ambition

David Robb and Ken Price love camping. Their ambition is to camp in every state in the U.S. They **1** *haven't done* (not do) that yet, but they're getting close. They **2** _____ _____ _____ (be) on three camping trips this summer. They just got back from the third one, and they **3** _____ (not change) their clothes _____ ! But they are ready to talk to me.

Me: How many states have you camped in so far?

David: Well, **4** I _____ (camp) in 33. Ken's only camped in 32.

Me: Do you think you will be famous?

David: We are famous! We **5** _____ _____ _____ (be) on TV twice! And Ken just spoke to a TV travel show presenter on the phone.

Me: Really?

David: Yes, about ten minutes ago.

Me: **6** _____ (you / meet) any famous people _____ ?

David: No. We **7** _____ (not meet) any famous people _____ .

Me: Where are you going on your next vacation?

David: Well, we **8** _____ (not be) to Texas _____ , so that's next. Camping in Texas!

Me: Good luck.

Use your English: Exclamations

4 ★ Cross out the response that is NOT correct.

1 **A:** Paul is usually late, but yesterday he arrived on time.
   B: *What a surprise! / ~~How awful!~~ / How nice!*

2 **A:** I can't go to the party. I have to babysit my sister.
   B: *That's great! / No way! / What a pity!*

3 **A:** I turned on my computer and nothing happened.
   B: *How weird! / You're kidding! / What a fantastic night!*

4 **A:** We saw the band and took photos of them.
   B: *How amazing! / That's incredible! / That's a shame.*

5 **A:** I was eating a burger and found a dead bug in it.
   B: *How disgusting! / How nice! / What a nightmare!*

6 **A:** I saw our teacher at school today, but he's not teaching us this class.
   B: *How disgusting! / How strange! / How weird!*

7 **A:** I did great on my English test.
   B: *That's great! / How amazing! / What a pity!*

Consolidation

5 Complete the conversations with the cues.

have / great / yet

Pam: I just got my grades.

Lucy: Have you looked at them **1** *yet*?

Pam: Yes, I **2** _____ . I passed everything.

Lucy: That's **3** _____ !

yet / already / kidding

Liam: I haven't had lunch **4** _____ . I haven't had time. I just finished a four-hour test.

Neil: You're **5** _____ !

Liam: No, I'm not. I've **6** _____ had three tests this week, and it's only Wednesday.

haven't / already / yet / nightmare

Jan: Have you watched the Jonas Brothers DVD **7** _____ ?

Marcela: No, I **8** _____ .

Jan: Why not? You've **9** _____ had it for three days.

Marcela: I know, but my DVD player isn't working.

Jan: What a **10** _____ !

He gave rock lessons.

Vocabulary: Types of music

1 ★ **Circle the ones that are types of music.**

1 (jazz)/ jars / jeans

2 heavy metal / deep metal / wide metal

3 class / classroom / classical

4 city / country / continent

5 stone / brick / rock

6 reggae / rugby / regret

7 rip / rap / rope

8 techno / technique / technical

9 sale / seal / soul

10 fork / folk / fake

11 Latin / Greek / Roman

12 B&B / M&M / R&B

Grammar: Simple past and present perfect

2 ★ **Write the verbs in parentheses in the correct form.**

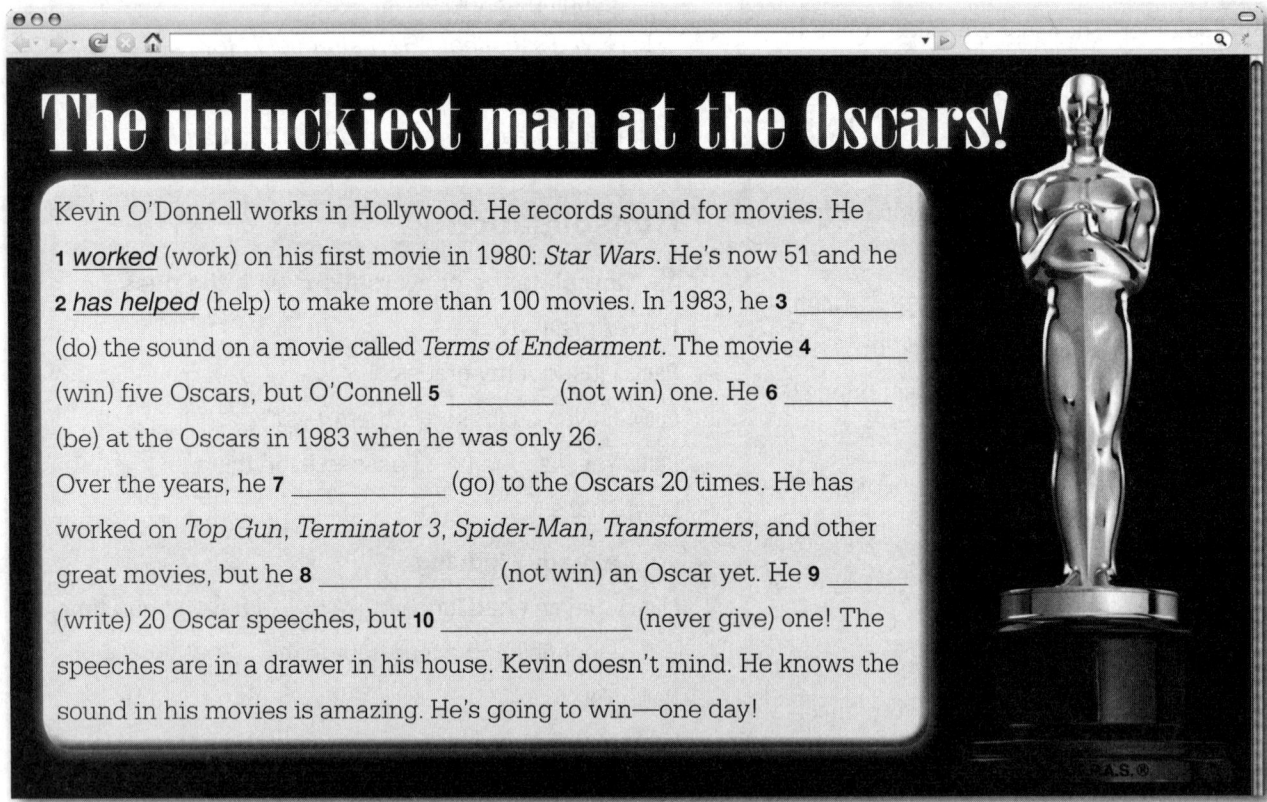

The unluckiest man at the Oscars!

Kevin O'Donnell works in Hollywood. He records sound for movies. He **1** _worked_ (work) on his first movie in 1980: *Star Wars*. He's now 51 and he **2** _has helped_ (help) to make more than 100 movies. In 1983, he **3** _____ (do) the sound on a movie called *Terms of Endearment*. The movie **4** _____ (win) five Oscars, but O'Connell **5** _____ (not win) one. He **6** _____ (be) at the Oscars in 1983 when he was only 26.

Over the years, he **7** _____ (go) to the Oscars 20 times. He has worked on *Top Gun*, *Terminator 3*, *Spider-Man*, *Transformers*, and other great movies, but he **8** _____ (not win) an Oscar yet. He **9** _____ (write) 20 Oscar speeches, but **10** _____ (never give) one! The speeches are in a drawer in his house. Kevin doesn't mind. He knows the sound in his movies is amazing. He's going to win—one day!

3 ★★ **Use sentence a, b, or c to write a correct sentence for each time expression.**

a) I went to the U.S.   b) I have won a contest.   c) Have you cooked dinner?

1 in 2004 I _went to the U.S. in 2004._

2 three months ago

_____

3 ever

_____

4 last week

_____

5 yesterday

_____

6 yet

_____

7 never

_____

Consolidation

4 Write conversations using the cues.

1 Tom: you / ever be / to a rock concert?

Matt: ✓

Tom: When / you / go?

Matt: I / go / in 2009

Tom: you / like it?

Matt: ✓ / It / be / great

Tom: *Have you ever been to a rock concert?*

Matt: *Yes, I have.*

Tom: *When did you go?*

Matt: *I went in 2009.*

Tom: *Did you like it?*

Matt: *Yes, I did. It was great.*

2 Sara: you / ever play / in a concert?

Mel: ✓

Sara: What instrument / you play?

Mel: I / play / the piano

Sara: you / make / any mistakes?

Mel: ✗

Sara: _____

Mel: _____

Sara: _____

Mel: _____

Sara: _____

Mel: _____

3 Cathy: your mom / ever go / to a rock festival?

Debbie: ✓

Cathy: When / she / go?

Debbie: She / go / in 1980

Cathy: What / she / look like then?

Debbie: She / have / short, pink hair

Cathy: _____

Debbie: _____

Cathy: _____

Debbie: _____

Cathy: _____

Debbie: _____

Extra challenge!

5 ★★★ Read the profiles and complete the information.

Shakira	
Style of music:	Latin pop (also rock, world, dance)
First record:	1990
Number of records in her life:	eight albums up to now
Awards:	two Grammy awards, seven Latin Grammy awards
Personal life:	engaged to Antonio de la Rua

Shakira is a *Latin pop* singer. She *made* her first record *in 1990*. She *has made* eight albums in her life. She *has won* two Grammy awards and seven Latin Grammy awards. She is *engaged to* Antonio de la Rua.

The Black Eyed Peas	
Group:	three men and a woman
Style of music:	hip-hop (also pop)
First record:	1998
Number of records:	six albums up to now
Awards:	six Grammy awards

The Black Eyed Peas are three **1** _____ and a **2** _____ . They play **3** _____ and **4** _____ music. They **5** _____ their first record **6** _____ _____ . They **7** _____ six albums altogether. The Black Eyed Peas **8** _____ already _____ six Grammy Awards.

CONSOLIDATION

The challenge

Before you read

1 Before you read, check the meaning of these words.

> **New words**
> • council • festival • newsletter • nervous • to raise (money)
> • representative • sponsored (*adj*) • volunteer (*n*)

A

From: **Becky**
To: **Kate**

Dear Kate,
The festival just ended. It was a sunny day and we raised over $400. A reporter from the local newspaper took our picture! I really enjoyed it. Next year, I'm going to organize something else with Darren. I don't know what yet.
Becky

B

From: **Becky**
To: **Kate**

Dear Kate,
I just went to my first school council meeting. I was the student representative for 9th grade. The teacher spoke first about the school newsletter. I didn't really listen—I was too nervous! Then we talked about school trips and after-school clubs. The teacher gave us all a challenge: to think of different ways to raise money for them. We talked and talked. In the end, we decided to have a sponsored walk and an outdoor festival. I'm going to organize the festival with a guy called Darren from 10th grade. He looks a little scary, but he's very nice.

Becky

C

From: **Becky**
To: **Kate**

Dear Kate,
The festival is on Saturday. We've done lots of work. We had lots of good ideas. People are going to bring cookies to sell, and we're going to sell old books and CDs, too. The PE teachers are going to organize some games, and my art teacher is going to do face-painting.
We found some volunteers from 9th and 10th grades to help us. It wasn't easy, because no one wants to come to school on a Saturday! We made some posters on the computer. Everyone took a poster home.
Darren has been really helpful—not scary at all. We're a great team! I hope everything is OK on Saturday!
Becky

Read

2 ★ Read the e-mails quickly and put them in the correct time order.

1 ____   2 ____   3 ____

3 ★ Match words (1–7) with words (a–g).

1 school _d_   a) newspaper
2 student ____   b) clubs
3 school ____   c) representative
4 sponsored ____   d) council
5 outdoor ____   e) trip
6 local ____   f) walk
7 after-school ____   g) festival

Becky

4 ★★ **Circle the correct answers.**

1 Becky is in 9th grade when she . . .

  a) joins the school council.

  b) works on the school newsletter.

2 The school needs money for . . .

  a) a festival.

  b) school trips and after-school activities.

3 Darren . . .

  a) is in the grade above Becky at school.

  b) is scary.

4 Becky . . .

  a) wasn't very confident at first.

  b) didn't want to organize a school festival.

5 Darren and Becky . . .

  a) worked well together.

  b) didn't want to ask anyone else for help.

6 The best description of the day is:

  a) It was a success, and Becky had a good time.

  b) It wasn't a success, but Becky had a good time.

Listen

> **Learning strategy: Pay attention to key words**
>
> **Remember!** When you listen or read, pay attention to key words. They often contain important information, and they are usually stressed.

5 ★ 🎧 10 **Listen to the first three lines of the recording and underline the words that are stressed.**

1 The <u>festival</u> was <u>really</u> <u>fun</u> last year.

2 Yes, we were a good team.

3 And we raised 400 dollars for the school.

6 ★★ 🎧 11 **Underline the key words in these sentences, then listen. Write *T* for *true*, *F* for *false*, or *NI* for *no information*.**

1 The <u>festival</u> was <u>really fun</u> last year. | T |

2 Darren wants to organize another festival. | |

3 Darren thinks Becky's idea is boring. | |

4 The DJ plays rap music. | |

5 Darren is too young to go to clubs. | |

6 People pay $25 to $50 for "buy a song." | |

7 People can pay for the DJ to stop playing a song, too. | |

Write

7 ★ **The dance was last night. Imagine you are Becky. Look at the notes. On a piece of paper, write a message to tell a friend what happened.**

This year's challenge: organize a dance and raise more money than last year
Started 8 P.M. - ended 11 P.M.
100 people
Raised $200 from tickets, $150 from snacks, $80 from "Buy a song"
Andy (DJ) - great; music - awesome!
Everyone - happy; me - excited and tired;
Darren - looked great - two dances with him
Saturday morning - Darren and I cleaned up.
Took four hours!

Dear Lucy,
I had a great time last Friday. Our school council challenge this year was to organize a dance. Guess what! I danced with a boy called Darren from 11th grade. It . . .

Hope all is well.
Love,
Becky

10A It will fly at 3,000 mph.

Grammar: *will* for predictions

1 ★ Match the beginnings of the sentences (1–10) to the endings (a–j).

Predictions for the year 2050

1 People will live __*d*__
2 We will fly ___
3 Someone will make ___
4 We will listen to ___
5 Everyone will work ___
6 There won't be any schools, so there won't be ___
7 Students will learn from ___
8 Countries won't fight ___
9 Lots of animals will disappear ___
10 Cars won't use ___

a) cell phones in our ears.
b) against other countries.
c) computers; they won't go to school.
d) on other planets.
e) at home.
f) gas any more.
g) from the world.
h) to the Moon.
i) any teachers.
j) a car that can fly, probably a Japanese company.

2 ★★ Complete the article with the correct form of the verbs.

Imagine the future . . .

In 20 years, everything **1** *will be* (be) different.
Computers **2** _____ (talk) to all the machines
in our kitchens. Refrigerators **3** _____ (have)
computers, too. You **4** _____ (not / go) to the
supermarket to buy food. You **5** _____ (tell)
the refrigerator what you want to eat, and the
refrigerator **6** _____ (know) what food to
buy. Your refrigerator **7** _____ (talk) to a
computer at the supermarket. After that, the food
8 _____ (arrive) at your house. How
9 _____ it _____ (come)? It **10** _____
(not / be) quick. A teenager **11** _____ (ride)
a bike to your house with your food! **12** _____
you _____ (know) what will happen in the
future? No one really knows, but it's fun to imagine!

Consolidation

3 Complete the conversation with the correct form of *will* and the verbs in parentheses.

Mark: What do you think the world **1** *will be* (be) like in 50 years? **2** _____ it _____ (be) a nice place?

Nathan: No, it **3** _____ .

Mark: No? Why not?

Nathan: It **4** _____ (be) dirty. People **5** _____ (not have) enough food.

Mark: But there **6** _____ (be) new ways to make food.

Nathan: And there **7** _____ (not be) any gas.

Mark: We **8** _____ (not need) oil. Cars and planes **9** _____ (use) solar energy.

Nathan: Oh, yes. The sun.

Mark: **10** _____ the world _____ (be) hotter?

Nathan: Yes, it **11** _____ .

Mark: What **12** _____ the temperature in the U.K. _____ (be) in the summer?

Nathan: It could be 95° Fahrenheit, or 35°C in the summer!

Mark: Ninety-five degrees in the U.K.? That isn't possible!

Extra challenge!

4 ★★★ Complete the quotes about the future by using *will* and the correct form of the verbs in parentheses and by guessing the missing words and checking your answers below.

1 *Rock'n'roll will be* (be) gone by June.
(*Variety* entertainment magazine, 1955)
a) the U.S.   b) Rock'n'Roll   c) Cars

2 _____ _____ (be) dead by 1950.
(John Langdon-Davies, journalist, 1936)
a) Democracy   b) Television   c) Movies

3 A rocket _____ (never be) able to _____ . (*New York Times*, 1936)
a) fly   b) travel to the Moon
c) leave the Earth's atmosphere

4 Man _____ (not fly) for _____ years.
(Wilbur Wright of the Wright Brothers, 1901)
a) ten   b) 50   c) 100

5 _____ _____ (not last).
(Darryl Zanuck, movie producer and director, 1946)
a) Television   b) The war   c) Communism

6 In the future, everyone _____ (be) famous for _____ . (Andy Warhol, artist, 1968)
a) a day   b) something   c) 15 minutes

If I have time, I'll show you.

Vocabulary: Computer language

1 ★ Complete the words.

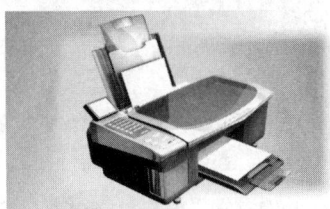

1 p*rinter*

2 s _ a _ _ e _

3 s _ r _ _ _

4 w _ _ s _ t _

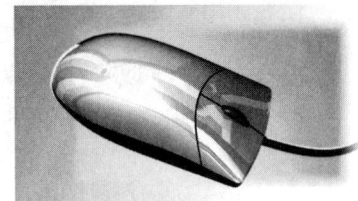

5 m _ _ s _

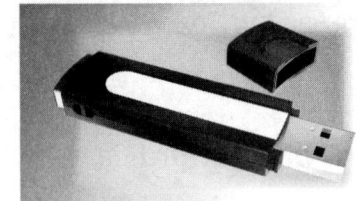

6 m _ m _ _ _ s _ i _ _

7 l _ _ t _ _

8 k _ y _ o a _ _

9 P _ (d _ _ k _ _ p c _ _ p _ _ _ _)

2 ★ ★ Complete the conversations with words from the box.

> • attachment • burn • crashed • delete • downloaded • Internet
> • open • quick • received • ~~send~~ • virus

Paolo: I got a letter from my mom this morning. She wants to know all about Seattle and our language school. I can't call her because my cell phone isn't working.

Luca: Why don't you **1** *send* her an e-mail from the Internet café? You can add an

2 _____ .

It has broadband so it will be very **3** _____ .

Rob: Mom, what are you doing?

Mom: I'm reading my e-mails. I just **4** _____ some new ones. This one looks interesting. I don't know who it's from.

Rob: Don't **5** _____ it, Mom. It could be a

6 _____ . **7** _____ it now.

Ben: I tried to **8** _____ a movie onto a DVD, but my computer **9** _____ and now it doesn't work.

Ana: What movie was it?

Ben: Some movie I **10** _____ from the **11** _____ . I found a good site for free movies.

Ana: You have to be careful. Not all sites are safe.

Grammar: Conditional: *if clause* + future

The automatic mouse catcher

3 ★ Look at the picture. Write the correct form of the verbs in parentheses.

1 If the mouse *eats* (eat) A, B *will break* (break).

2 If B _____ (break), C _____ (fall) onto D.

3 If C _____ (fall) onto D, D _____ (play) music.

4 If D _____ (play) music, E _____ (wake up).

5 If E _____ (wake up), it _____
_____ (start) to sing.

6 If E _____ (start) to sing, G _____ (hear) it.

7 If G _____ (hear) E, it _____ (jump)
onto F and _____ (see) the mouse.

8 If G _____ (see) the mouse, it _____ (jump)
down and _____ (catch) the mouse.

4 ★★ Write questions about what will happen in Exercise 3 using the cues.

1 What / happen / a mouse / eat / this cheese?

What will happen if a mouse eats the cheese?

B will break.

2 Where / C fall / B / break?

_____

It will fall on D.

3 E / wake up / the music / start ?

_____

Yes, it will.

4 G / catch / the mouse / E / not start to sing?

_____

No, it won't.

Consolidation

5 Complete the conversation using the appropriate words and the correct form of the verbs in parentheses.

Mom: This old computer is awful.

Will: Buy a new one.

Mom: 1 *If* I *buy* (buy) a new computer, what
2 _____ I _____ (do) with the old one?

Will: Give it to Jack.

Mom: No, 3 _____ Jack _____ (have) a
computer in his bedroom, we 4 _____
(not see) him. Anyway, if I get a new computer,
what 5 _____ (happen) to all my work?

Will: Don't worry. I'll help you. It's easy.

Mom: 6 _____ your dad's old games
_____ (work) on a new computer?

Will: No, 7 _____ . But if you get
a new computer, I 8 _____ (find)
him some new games. I 9 _____
(download) some from the Internet.

Mom: 10 _____ I _____ (buy) a black
computer, 11 _____ it
_____ (look) nice in here?

Will: Yes, 12 _____ (look) very nice. And I
think a new computer will look very nice in my
bedroom, too!

10c I'll be more careful.

Grammar: *will* for decisions/promises; *will* for offers

1 ★ Match the problems (1–8) to the decisions or promises (a–h).

1 My hands are dirty. *h*

2 My laptop doesn't work. ___

3 My batteries are dead. ___

4 My blue skirt is torn. ___

5 There isn't any food in the refrigerator. ___

6 Jamie has my new video game. ___

7 My mom isn't very well. ___

8 I'm sorry. I broke your pen. ___

a) I'll charge them before I go out.

b) I'll call him and get it back.

c) I'll make her a cup of tea.

d) I'll wear the red one.

e) I'll buy you a new one.

f) I'll call out for a pizza.

g) I'll take it to the computer store this afternoon.

h) I'll wash them before I eat.

2 ★ Complete the conversations with 'll and the verbs.

1 A: My laptop doesn't work.

   B: I*'ll look* (look) at it for you.

2 A: I need something to drink.

   B: I_____ (make) some coffee.

3 A: I don't understand this homework.

   B: I_____ (help) you.

4 A: I'm bored.

   B: I_____ (lend) you a magazine.

5 A: It's my birthday on Saturday.

   B: I_____ (make) you a cake.

6 A: I'm having problems at school.

   B: I_____ (talk) to your teacher if you like.

7 A: I'll meet you in the restaurant in five minutes.

   B: OK. I_____ (order) some food.

3 ★★ Complete the conversation using the cues.

Emma: This is a great store. I'm going to buy some jeans.

Trish: 1 I / get / sales clerk

   I'll get a sales clerk.

Emma: OK. I'm going to the dressing room now.

Trish: 2 I / hold your bag

   _____

Emma: Great, thanks.

***

Emma: They're too tight.

Trish: 3 If / you / want / I / find / a bigger pair for you.

   _____

Emma: Thanks.

***

Emma: They're great. Oh, no. I left my money at home.

Trish: 4 If / you / need / money / I / lend / some.

   _____

Emma: Thanks, you're a real friend.

***

Emma: Oh, no! I missed the bus!

Trish: 5 I / walk home with you / if / you / want

   _____

Emma: Great. Thanks for everything!

Trish: No problem.

Vocabulary: Problems

4 ★ Complete the sentences using the correct adjectives.

1 He has a **cracked** face.

He has a *dirty* face.

2 The shirt is **dead**.

The shirt is _____ .

3 This cup is **torn**.

This cup is _____ .

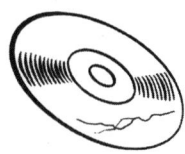

4 My CD is **missing**.

My CD is _____ .

5 Oh, no! My guitar is **scratched**.

Oh, no! My guitar is _____ .

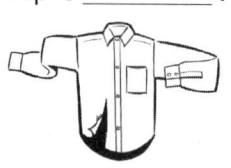

6 I can't wear this. It's **dirty**.

I can't wear this. It's _____ .

7 My cell phone is **stained**.

My cell phone is _____ .

8 My batteries don't work. They're **broken**.

My batteries don't work. They're _____ .

Use your English: Describe and deal with problems

5 ★ Circle the correct words.

Boy: I have a **1** (*problem*)/ *wrong* / *matter* with my cell phone.

Sales clerk: What's **2** *problem* / *wrong* / *matter* with it?

Boy: It doesn't **3** *look* / *right* / *work*. I can't hear anything on it.

Sales clerk: **4** *I* / *I'll* / *will* look at it.

Boy: Yes, please. That **5** *would* / *is* / *does* be great.

Sales clerk: Hmm. Oh, no.

Boy: What's the **6** *wrong* / *matter* / *repair* with it?

Sales clerk: It's **7** *wrong* / *cracked* / *problem*. Look. And the battery is **8** *charged* / *dead* / *work*. We can **9** *repair* / *work* / *look* it for you if you **10** *think* / *like* / *look*.

Boy: That's really **11** *kind* / *right* / *great* of you. Thank you.

Consolidation

6 Number the sentences in the correct order to make conversations.

A

1	a) Look at this CD.
	b) It's dirty.
	c) No, don't worry. I can do it.
	d) What's the matter with it?
	e) I'll clean it for you.

B

	a) That's great, thanks.
	b) I'll lend you mine if you want.
	c) No problem.
	d) My phone isn't working.
1	e) What's the problem?

C

1	a) What's wrong?
	b) Thanks.
	c) My best shirt is torn.
	d) It's not too bad. I can repair it.
	e) I'll look at it.

INTEGRATED
CONSOLIDATION
SKILLS

I hated it!

Before you read

1 Before you read, check the meaning of these words.

> **New words**
> * anywhere • atlas • out of date • papers
> * reference books • to survive • to turn on / off

Read

2 ★ Read the article and match the headings (a–e) to the paragraphs (1–5).

a) No computer for two days.

b) Never again!

c) ~~Homework wasn't as easy.~~

d) I used my phone more.

e) I didn't want to listen to them talking!

No computer day!

How did you survive?

1 ☐ *c* **Ben, Seattle, Washington**
It was very hard. I had a lot of homework to do. Usually, I use the computer to find information, and I write my papers on it. My dad has lots of books, atlases, and reference books, but almost all of them are out of date! It wasn't difficult to find information, but it took more time.

2 ☐ **Jenny, Des Moines, Iowa**
I couldn't chat online with my friends. I hated it! I sent a lot of texts. A few of my friends also turned off their computers, but most of them didn't. On Sunday, there were lots of messages to read.

3 ☐ **David, Los Angeles, California**
I usually listen to sports on the Internet on Saturdays. I can listen to baseball from anywhere in the U.S. or soccer from Europe. I listened to my mom's small kitchen radio. It was awful. There was no soccer at all. I won't join in the next "no computer" day!

4 ☐ **Sara, Orlando, Florida**
My main problem was music. The battery in my cell phone was dead. I don't have a CD player or DVD player—only on my computer—so I listened to the radio. It wasn't very good. A few DJs are OK, but most of them talk too much.

5 ☐ **Lisa, Houston, Texas**
I read a lot. My mom has some good books. It was very relaxing. Usually, my eyes hurt at night. Last Saturday, they were fine. I went to bed earlier, too. The next day, I didn't turn on my computer at all. I wanted to finish my book.

3 ★★ **Read the article again and complete the sentences.**

1 Ben: "It's quicker to do *homework* on the *computer*."

2 Jenny: "Only a _____ of my _____ turned off their computers."

3 David: "My mom's radio didn't have _____ from _____ on it."

4 Sara: "Why do radio _____ _____ so much?"

5 Lisa: "My _____ didn't _____ at all at night."

Listen

4 ★ (12) **Listen. Then circle the correct answers.**

1 The students use computers . . .
  a) one day a week.
  b) twice a week.
  c) only for foreign languages.

2 The girl doesn't like . . .
  a) French.
  b) computers.
  c) using the computer to learn French.

3 The French teacher can . . .
  a) hear what the students are saying.
  b) see what websites the students are looking at.
  c) shout loudly.

4 In the other computer class, students . . .
  a) do project work.
  b) make websites.
  c) work alone.

5 Students use the computers to . . .
  a) find information.
  b) plan what to write.
  c) talk to the teacher.

6 The students . . .
  a) often look at funny websites in class.
  b) didn't look at a funny website for long.
  c) showed a funny website to their teacher.

Write

> **Writing tip: Quantifiers: *all, most, some, a few***
> **Remember!** We use quantifiers such as *all, most, some,* and *a few* to talk in general terms about numbers of people or things.
> Almost **all teenagers** have a computer.
> **Most teenagers** use the computer to send e-mails.
> **Some teenagers** use instant messaging.
> **A few teenagers** use their computers to shop online.

5 ★ **Look at these facts about computers and students and complete the sentences.**

> 100% of students have computer classes.
> 95% of students like computer classes.
> 75% of students work hard in computer classes.
> 40% of teachers never use computers in class.
> 10% of students send personal e-mails in computer classes.

1 Some *teachers never use computers in class*.
2 A few _____ .
3 All _____ .
4 Most _____ .
5 Almost all _____ .

6 ★★ **On a piece of paper, write a paragraph about computers at your school. Think about these things:**

- Do all students have computer classes?
- Do students enjoy computer classes?
- Do teachers know how to use computers?
- Do students talk about their favorite websites?
- Do students work hard in computer classes?
- Do students use school computers in their free time?

81

Phrases

1 ★ Circle the correct responses.

1 That's a nice TV.

  a) Yes, but it cost a ton!

  b) Yes, I've always wanted to.

  c) Yes, with a little luck.

2 It's going to be a perfect day for the beach.

  a) Yes, I'll be fine.   b) Yes, with a little luck.

  c) Yes, I hate to say this.

3 We're going to Cancún for our vacation.

  a) I can't wait!   b) I hate to say this.

  c) I'll be fine.

4 I hate to say this, but . . .

  a) that's great, thank you.   b) don't worry.

  c) I lost the tickets.

Vocabulary: Illness

2 ★ Complete the sentences with words from the box.

• burn • cough • headache • hurts • pain • sick • stomachache • temperature • toothache

1 Ow! Be careful with that coffee . . . Look, now I have a _burn_ on my arm.

2 Rob has a _____ of 102.°

3 Don't eat so quickly. You'll get a _____ .

4 I have some _____ in my back. I'm going to lie down.

5 That's a bad _____ . Why don't you have a glass of water?

6 A: I have a _____ .

  B: Why don't you call the dentist?

7 I feel _____ . Quick, I have to get to the bathroom!

8 My arm _____ after that game of tennis.

9 A: I have a _____ .

  B: That's because you watch too much TV!

Grammar: *should/shouldn't*

3 ★ Complete the paragraph with *should* or *shouldn't* and the correct form of the verbs.

My friend, Raul, has had a few problems with his health. He wasn't feeling well, so he told his parents. His mom said: "You **1** _should eat_ (eat) more vegetables. You **2** _____ (not eat) fast food every day." His dad said: "You **3** _____ (go) to bed earlier. You **4** _____ (not stay) up so late at night." He called me and told me about his problems. I said: "You **5** _____ (not play) so many video games. You **6** _____ (go) outside and play soccer." He didn't go to school last week. He went to see the doctor. The doctor said: "You **7** _____ (stay) at home for a week. You **8** _____ (not go) out, and you **9** _____ (not use) your computer." At school today, Raul looked sad. Our teacher asked him: "What's wrong? You **10** _____ (be) happy. You weren't here last week." Raul is doing all his school work from last week. He's not happy at all!

4 ★★ Write questions and answers about Raul using the cues.

1 we / take away his computer? (✗)

A: *Should we take away his computer?*

B: *No, you shouldn't.*

2 What time / he / go to bed? (9 P.M.)

A: *What time should he go to bed?*

B: *He should go to bed at 9 P.M.*

3 What / he / eat? (more vegetables)

A: _____

_____

B: _____

_____

4 he / play more video games? (✗)

A: _____

_____

B: _____

_____

5 Raul / give his eyes a rest? (✓)

A: _____

_____

B: _____

_____

6 What school work / he do? (everything we did last week)

A: _____

_____

B: _____

_____

7 I / take Raul to a fast-food restaurant? (✗)

A: _____

_____

B: _____

_____

8 we / be worried? (✗)

A: _____

_____

B: _____

_____

Use your English: Say what the matter is and give advice

5 ★ Number the sentences in the correct order to make a conversation.

☐1 a) **Cathy:** You don't look very well. Are you OK?

☐ b) **Cathy:** You shouldn't eat so much at night.

☐ c) **Cathy:** Oh, no. How long have you had that?

☐ d) **Ellie:** I know. What should I do now?

☐ e) **Ellie:** No. I have a stomachache.

☐ f) **Cathy:** So take some medicine for your stomach and go to bed.

☐ g) **Ellie:** I don't like going to the doctor.

☐ h) **Ellie:** It started last night. I ate a big Chinese meal.

☐ i) **Cathy:** You should go to the doctor.

☐10 j) **Ellie:** Good idea.

Consolidation

6 Complete the conversation with words from the box.

> • a ton • have • hurt • luck • shouldn't • take • this • to

James: I have a new computer. It cost **1** *a ton*.

Henry: Wow, it's great! I've always wanted **2** _____ have a screen like this. Let's play some games.

Five hours later:

James: Do you want to play another game?

Henry: I hate to say **3** _____ , but I think I should stop. I **4** _____ a really bad headache.

James: Oh. Do you want to **5** _____ an aspirin?

Henry: No, it's OK.

James: OK. Do you want to watch a DVD?

Henry: No! I'd like to, but I know I **6** _____ look at any more screens. My eyes **7** _____ . I'm going home.

James: OK. See you tomorrow. I'm going to play another game. With a little **8** _____ , I'll beat my high score.

Henry: If you play now, you'll get a really bad headache, too! Bye!

Vocabulary: Household chores

1 ★ Complete the words.

1 c*lean*_____

2 i_____

3 g__ s_____

4 d__ t__ __
l_____

5 d__ t__ __
d_____

6 v_____

7 c_____

2 ★★ Complete the sentences with the correct form of a verb from the box.

> • clean • clean • empty • ~~make~~ • make • make • set
> • take • wash • wash

1 Why didn't you *make* your bed this morning?

2 I can't come out now. I'm _____ the house.

3 Could you _____ the dishwasher and put the dishes away?

4 I _____ breakfast yesterday. You should _____ it today.

5 Look at this can! Please _____ the garbage out now.

6 Mom, I've _____ my room. Can I go out now?

7 Chris, please _____ the table. It's nearly dinnertime.

8 Dad is _____ the car. He always _____

the car on Sunday morning.

Grammar: *have to/don't have to*

3 ★ Complete the sentences. Use the information in the ad.

Sunny Beach Summer Camp

needs workers:

Four cleaners
1 cleaning the restaurant
3 washing the uniforms
5 cleaning the rooms
7 doing the vacuuming
9 ironing the uniforms

One kitchen assistant
2 setting the tables
4 doing the dishes
6 making breakfast
8 emptying the dishwasher
10 helping the cooks

1 The cleaners *have to clean* the restaurant.

2 The kitchen assistant *has to set* the tables.

3 The cleaners first _____ the uniforms.

4 The kitchen assistant _____ the dishes.

5 The cleaners _____ the rooms.

6 The kitchen assistant _____ breakfast.

7 The cleaners _____ the vacuuming.

8 The kitchen assistant _____ the dishwasher.

9 The cleaners _____ the uniforms.

10 The kitchen assistant _____ the cooks.

4 ★★ **Use the information in Exercise 3 to say what the people don't have to do.**

1 The kitchen assistant *doesn't have to clean the restaurant*.

2 The cleaners *don't have to set the tables* .

3 The kitchen assistant _____ .

4 The cleaners _____ .

5 The kitchen assistant _____ .

6 The cleaners _____ .

7 The kitchen assistant _____ .

8 The cleaners _____ .

9 The kitchen assistant _____ .

10 The cleaners _____ .

5 ★★ **Ellie is talking to someone from the summer camp. Complete her questions.**

Ellie: Hello, I'm calling about the jobs at your summer camp.

Man: Oh, yes. What would you like to know?

Ellie: 1 the kitchen assistant / speak / foreign language?

Does the kitchen assistant have to speak a foreign language?

Man: No. All our workers speak English.

Ellie: 2 the kitchen assistant / know / how to cook?

_____

Man: No. The cook does all the cooking.

Ellie: 3 What time / cleaners / start in the morning?

_____

Man: They have to start at 6 A.M.

Ellie: 4 How many days a week they / work?

_____

Man: They have to work five days a week. Everyone has to work on Saturday and Sunday.

Ellie: 5 the kitchen assistant / wear a uniform?

_____

Man: Yes, all our workers have to wear a uniform.

Ellie: 6 When / apply for the job?

_____

Man: You have to apply before April 25.

Ellie: 7 I / send a letter?

_____

Man: No, you don't. You can send an e-mail.

Ellie: OK. Thank you very much.

Man: You're welcome.

Consolidation

6 **Circle the correct choices.**

1 Do you have to do _____?

 a) your room   b) your bed   c) the dishes

2 Where _____ your father have to go today?

 a) does   b) is   c) has

3 What _____ you have to wear to school?

 a) are   b) does   c) do

4 Do you have to _____ the garbage out?

 a) take   b) make   c) empty

5 What time do you have to _____ up?

 a) getting   b) to get   c) get

6 I _____ have to make breakfast every day.

 a) don't   b) haven't   c) 'm not

7 "Does your sister have to set the table?"
 "Yes, she _____ ."

 a) has   b) sets   c) does

8 "Do you have to wash the car?" "No, I _____ ."

 a) haven't   b) don't   c) 'm not

Grammar: *had to/didn't have to*

1 ★ **Complete the message with the correct form of *have to* and the verbs in parentheses.**

Dear Vicky,

I had a great summer, but it was tiring. I was working in a coffee shop. It was fun, but hard work. I **1** *had to get up* (✓ get up) at six o'clock every morning. Then I **2** _____ (✓ walk) a mile to the coffee shop. There aren't any buses, and my mom and dad didn't want to get up so early! I **3** _____ (✗ not do) any cooking, but I **4** _____ (✓ set) the tables. After breakfast, I **5** _____ (✓ do) the dishes and then I **6** _____ (✗ do) anything until lunchtime. I usually went home, but sometimes I met friends downtown. In the afternoons, I **7** _____ (✓ work) for three hours and then I worked again at night. I finished at nine o'clock, but I **8** _____ (✗ walk) home—my dad came to get me and drove me home. I was sad to leave. I **9** _____ (✓ leave) because school starts next week, but I can work there on Saturdays, which is great. How was your summer?

See you soon.

Love

Cathy

2 ★★ **Write the questions and answers about Cathy. Use the information from Exercise 1. Follow the examples.**

1 A: What time *did she have to get up*?

  B: She *had to get up* at 6 A.M.

2 A: *Did she have to do* any cooking?

  B: *No, she didn't* .

3 A: How far _____

   _____ ?

  B: She _____

   _____ .

4 A: _____

   _____

   the tables?

  B: _____ .

5 A: What _____

   _____ after breakfast?

  B: After breakfast, she _____

   _____ .

6 A: How long _____

   _____ in the afternoon?

  B: She _____

   _____

   in the afternoon.

7 A: _____

   _____ home at night?

  B: _____ .

8 A: Why _____

   _____ the coffee shop?

  B: She _____

   _____

   because _____

   _____ next week.

3 ★★ **Complete the text with the correct simple past forms of *have to* and verbs from the box.**

> • buy • call • carry • help
> • not look • pay • sit • walk
> • not work

Josh: I **1** *had to buy* a new computer last weekend because my old one broke, and I **2** _____ _____ it home because my parents were busy.

Maggie: Wow! **3** _____ you _____ all the way home?

Josh: No, I took a bus some of the way, but I was still tired when I got home. I **4** _____ down and have a drink of water before I opened the box.

Maggie: Did the new computer work OK?

Josh: Well, I had a few problems. I **5** _____ my friend Mark and ask him for help. I was lucky. He usually helps his dad in their store on Saturdays, but he **6** _____ _____ last Saturday, so he came over.

Maggie: 7 _____ you _____ him?

Josh: No. He did everything. He likes working alone. He says it's easier. He **8** _____ at any directions or anything. He knew exactly what to do.

Maggie: 9 _____ you _____ him?

Josh: No! He didn't want any money. He loves working with computers.

Consolidation

4 **Put the words in the correct sentence order.**

1 summer / in / had / English / read / last / We / three / to / books
   We had to read three books in English last summer.

2 all / Thursday / had / My / night / to / dad / work / last
   _____
   _____

3 week / the / have / your / doctor's / Did / to / last / to / mom / go
   _____
   _____

4 stay / station / long / at / police / have / How / the / to / you / did
   _____
   _____

5 have / hotel / We / for / to / breakfast / didn't / at / pay / our
   _____
   _____

6 didn't / wait / have / airport / long / I / at / to / the
   _____
   _____

7 you / last / clean / night / room / have / Did / your / to
   _____
   _____

Extra challenge!

5 ★★★ **Look at the notes. On a piece of paper, write what Sam has to / doesn't have to do now and what Sam's dad had to do / didn't have to do when he was young.**

1 *Sam has to get up at 6 A.M. on school days.*
   Sam's dad didn't have to get up at 6 A.M. on school days.

	Sam	Sam's dad
1 Get up at 6 A.M.	✓	X
2 Wear shorts to school	X	✓
3 Make breakfast	✓	X
4 Go to bed at 9 P.M.	✓	X
5 Wash the car every weekend	X	✓
6 Do lots of homework	✓	X
7 Help with the shopping	✓	X

First aid

Before you read

1 Before you read, check the meaning of these words.

New words
• boiling • handkerchief • to spill • to tie

1 ☐ My friend, Carlos, had a little accident at home the other day. He was making a cup of coffee when he spilled some boiling water on his arm. He didn't know what to do. He went to the refrigerator and found some butter. He put this on the burn. It was the wrong thing to do. The butter made the burn worse. You should run cold water on a burn.

2 ☐ My cousin, Angie, had the flu. She felt very hot. At first, she stayed in bed, but opened her bedroom windows. She didn't feel better, so she got up and went for a walk. She didn't wear a coat or a scarf. She felt good at first in the cold air, but when she got home, she was really ill. Her temperature went up to over 102° F (38.8° C). Her mom called the doctor. The doctor saw her and told her to stay in bed for a week.

3 ☐ My brother, Manuel, fell and cut himself on an old broken bottle in the neighborhood park. It wasn't a big cut. He tied a handkerchief around his leg and then played soccer with his friends. When he came home, he put a bandage on it. He didn't wash it or put any antiseptic cream on it. He took the bandage off the next day. His leg looked horrible. Mom took him to the doctor's. The doctor cleaned the cut and put a bandage on Manuel's leg. He put him on antibiotics, too. Now Manuel can't play sports for a month.

2 Write the words from the box in the correct group.

> • antibiotics • ~~antiseptic cream~~ • bandage
> • boiling water • broken bottle • butter • coat
> • cold water • ~~to fall~~ • flu • to go for a walk • scarf
> • to spill • to stay in bed • temperature • to wash

verbs *to fall* , _____ , _____ ,

_____ , _____ ,

nouns *antiseptic cream* , _____ ,

_____ , _____ , _____ ,

_____ , _____ , _____ ,

_____ , _____

Read

> **Learning strategy: Skim for gist**
> **Remember!** When you want to get an idea of
> what a text is about, you can skim it. Look at the
> headings in the text. Then read quickly and look
> for key words. These are usually nouns and verbs.

3 ★ Read the articles in Exercise 1 quickly
and underline the words (or forms of the words)
from Exercise 2. Then write the letter for the
correct heading of each article in the boxes
provided on page 88.

a) Always clean the cut

b) Put it on bread, not a burn

c) Wrong to go out

4 ★★ Read the articles again. Write *T* for *true*,
F for *false*, or *NI* for *no information*.

1 Carlos burned his arm. `T`

2 He found some butter on the table. ☐

3 The butter didn't make his arm feel better. ☐

4 Angie's bedroom was very hot. ☐

5 Angie went for a walk because she felt better. ☐

6 After the walk, Angie's temperature went up. ☐

7 Manuel wasn't worried when he cut himself. ☐

8 There wasn't any antiseptic cream in
the house. ☐

9 Manuel's leg looked better the next day. ☐

Listen

5 ★ 🎧 13 Listen to a doctor talking to five
patients. Circle the correct problems.

1 (a) the flu   b) a burn   c) a headache

2 a) stomachache   b) a nosebleed   c) burn

3 a) a cut   b) fainting   c) a sprain

4 a) a burn   b) a nosebleed   c) a bee sting

5 a) fainting   b) the flu   c) a headache

6 ★★ 🎧 13 Listen again and write the number
of the conversation (1–5) for each piece of
advice (a–e).

a) The patient should sit in a strange position. ☐

b) The patient must make sure it isn't dirty. ☐

c) The speaker should remember that she isn't
in a movie. ☐

d) The patient should be careful not to get cold. `1`

e) The patient shouldn't use any creams. ☐

Write

7 ★ Your friend has the flu. On a piece of
paper, write her a message with some advice.
Use the notes to help you.

go out ✗
go to bed ✓
drink lots of water ✓
check temperature ✓
keep warm ✓
open the windows ✗
do any housework ✗
rest ✓

Start like this:
Hi, Stella,
*Sorry to hear that you are sick. Don't worry. I had
the flu last week, and I'm much better now. This is
the advice the doctor gave me. You should . . .*

Finish like this:
Get better soon.
Love . . .

To help the environment

Vocabulary: Containers and materials

1 ★ Label the pictures with one word from each box.

| • cardboard • glass • glass • metal • paper |
| • plastic |

| • bag • bag • bottle • box • box • jar |

 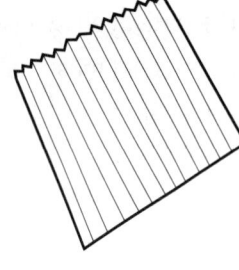

1 It's a *cardboard box* . 2 It's a _____
_____ .

3 It's a _____ 4 It's a _____
_____ . _____ .

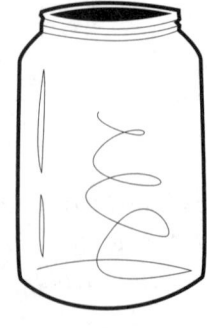 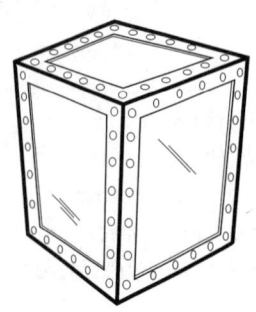

5 It's a _____ 6 It's a _____
_____ . _____ .

2 ★★ Complete the words.

1 Do you know what kind of m <u>e t a l</u> is used to make soda c <u>a n s</u> ?

2 To help the environment, I always use my own p _ _ _ _ _ _ b _ _ _ when I go to the supermarket.

3 I keep all my important papers in a big, heavy, m _ _ _ _ b _ _ in the attic.

4 Children love playing with c _ _ _ _ _ _ _ _ b _ _ _ _ .

5 I dropped my b _ _ _ _ _ of water. Luckily, it wasn't a g _ _ _ _ one, so it didn't break.

6 I never throw away p _ _ _ _ _ _ yogurt c _ _ _ _ _ _ _ _ _ _ . I wash them and reuse them.

Grammar: Infinitives of purpose

3 ★ Match the beginnings of the sentences (1–8) to the endings (a–h).

1 ~~My dad buys a newspaper~~ _c_
2 I study hard _____
3 My brother turned on his computer _____
4 Your parents went shopping _____
5 I sent a text to my friend _____
6 My friends always meet at the mall after school _____
7 Mark ran all the way home _____
8 My parents sometimes text me _____

| a) to surf the net. |
| b) to escape from an angry dog! |
| c) to read about problems in town. |
| d) to tell her about my party. |
| e) to ask me what I'm doing. |
| f) to get good grades in my classes. |
| g) to buy snacks and chat. |
| h) to buy you a birthday present. |

4 ★★ **Complete the text with the correct form of the verbs from the box.**

- carry • ~~do~~ • get • help • recycle • save
- stop • tell

My family cares about the environment. Yesterday, my dad went to the local supermarket **1** *to do* the weekly shopping.

He went there by bike **2** _____ on gas. He also took some bottles **3** _____ in the bottle return. We like our local supermarket because it doesn't use plastic bags. This is **4** _____ the environment. My dad took a reusable cloth bag **5** _____ his groceries in.

There is one problem, though. There are always lots of ads and coupons **6** _____ customers about special offers at the supermarket, but they are all over the ground.

My dad always talks to Joe outside the supermarket. Joe stands there all day **7** _____ people from taking things out of the supermarket without paying for them. Joe always watches my dad's bike, too, when he goes to the ATM **8** _____ money. Dad thinks Joe should pick up the ads and coupons!

Consolidation

5 **Circle the correct choices.**

Nina: Are we ready for the party?

Andy: I think so. I have some **1** (*cans*) / *bags* of soda.

Nina: Good. Do you have any water?

Andy: Yes. Five **2** *jars* / *bottles* .

Nina: **3** *Glass* / *Paper* or plastic?

Andy: Plastic. I got plastic ones **4** *to be* / *be* safe. I don't want anything to break. For food, I have ten **5** *cans* / *bags* of chips and a big tin of cookies.

Nina: A tin?

Andy: Yes, a big **6** *glass* / *metal* tin of cookies. My parents bought them **7** *gave* / *to give* to someone as a present, but they forgot! Oh yes, I have a DJ, too.

Nina: A DJ? Why?

Andy: **8** *Plays* / *To play* music, of course!

Nina: Yes, I know what a DJ does, but why do we need one?

Andy: Well, we need a DJ **9** *will give* / *to give* us time to relax. I don't want to spend all night worrying about CDs.

Nina: Good idea. And I have ten big **10** *cardboard* / *plastic* bags to put the garbage in after the party.

Andy: Oh yes, I forgot about that.

Nina: Yes, I thought so!

Vocabulary: Wild animals and insects

1 ★ **Circle the letter of the correct animals or insects.**

1 It can't fly.

   a) wasp   b) fly   c) spider   d) mosquito

2 It doesn't live on land.

   a) lion   b) dolphin   c) gorilla   d) giraffe

3 It can't swim.

   a) crocodile   b) rhino   c) shark   d) whale

4 It isn't a cat.

   a) cheetah   b) leopard   c) tiger   d) giraffe

5 Its babies come from eggs.

   a) snake   b) whale   c) gorilla   d) elephant

6 It doesn't eat meat.

   a) zebra   b) lion   c) shark   d) cheetah

7 It's bigger than a cat.

   a) hippo   b) fly   c) mosquito   d) wasp

Grammar: *so + adjective + that*

2 ★ **Complete the sentences using *so . . . that* and the adjectives in parentheses.**

1 My dog is *so smart that* (smart) he knows when it's time to go out.

2 Dan is _____ (lazy) he never studies.

3 My friends are _____ (nice) they bought me a present when I was sick.

4 Our school lunches are _____ (bad) everyone brings their own sandwiches.

5 The test was _____ (difficult) the highest grade was 63%.

6 The movie was _____ (scary) my little brother started to cry.

7 My dad is _____ (tired) in the mornings _____ he can't get out of bed.

8 My sister is _____ (intelligent) she is going to study at Harvard University next year.

3 ★★ **Combine the sentences using *so . . . that*.**

1 Ants are strong. They can carry very heavy weights.

   Ants are so strong that they can carry very heavy weights.

2 Giraffes are tall. They can eat leaves from very high trees.

   _____

   _____

3 Elephants are dangerous. They kill about 200 people in India every year.

   _____

   _____

4 Cheetahs are fast. They can catch any animal.

   _____

   _____

5 Male lions are lazy. The females have to hunt for all the food.

   _____

   _____

6 Chimpanzees are smart. They can remember numbers.

   _____

   _____

Consolidation

4 **Complete the conversation. Use words from the box.**

> • cheetahs • chimpanzees • dangerous • safe
> • ~~so~~ • so • spiders • that • wasp

Guide: Welcome to our zoo. It's **1** _so_ new that you are the first group to visit us. First, we're going to look at the big cats: tigers, lions, leopards, and **2** _____ .

Boy: It's not very nice for them in the zoo.

Guide: This zoo is very big and they have room to run around. They are so **3** _____ and happy here that they can live for 15 years. In Africa, they only live for about 7 years. After the cats, we're going to visit the monkey house. You must be careful there. The **4** _____ look friendly, but they can be very dangerous. They are so strong **5** _____ they can break your arm in a second.

Boy: Where are we going after that?

Guide: To the hot house. Dangerous animals like crocodiles, **6** _____ , and snakes live in the hot house. The green mamba snake is so **7** _____ that it can kill in seconds.

Boy: Is it safe in there?

Guide: Oh, yes. Don't worry. The glass walls are **8** _____ strong that nothing can break them. This is a very safe zoo.

Boy: Ow!

Guide: What was that?

Boy: A **9** _____ . It stung me. This zoo isn't safe! It's dangerous!

Extra challenge!

5 ★★★ **Match the animals (a–f) to the correct sentences (1–6).**

1 This animal gives children rides. [a]

2 We grew some trees to let this animal play. ☐

3 We had to build a very big house to give this animal room to move. ☐

4 We sent this animal to another zoo to save money on meat. ☐

5 We put this animal a long way from the trees to stop it from eating all the leaves. ☐

6 We built a big pool to let this animal swim around. ☐

12c I'd prefer to watch.

Phrases

1 ★ Combine the words to make the phrases. Then use them to complete the sentences.

Don't be	looks	a wimp
give it	such	try
it	a	it
up	for	awesome

1 A: I'm not going to go swimming here.

B: Come on. *Don't be such a wimp*!

A: I'm not scared; I just don't think we should.

2 A: Hey, guys. I don't know if I can do this.

B: Well, _____ and see.

3 A: Does anyone want to go climbing this weekend?

B: Yes, I'm _____ .

C: Me, too.

4 A: This is the castle we visited.

B: You're so lucky! _____ !

Grammar: *would ('d) rather; would ('d) prefer*

2 ★ Complete the sentences with words from the box.

| 'd • not • or • prefer • rather • than |

1 I*'d* rather play baseball than football.

2 We'd _____ to go to the movies.

3 Would you _____ go shopping?

4 I'd prefer _____ to play video games. I don't like them.

5 Would you rather swim _____ sunbathe?

6 She'd rather watch TV _____ surf the net.

3 ★★ Complete the sentences about the pictures using verbs and the words in parentheses.

1 Mark *would prefer to watch* TV. (prefer)

Cathy *would rather play* volleyball. (rather)

2 My dad _____ pizza. (prefer)

My mom _____ dinner. (rather)

3 My uncle _____ to town. (rather)

My aunt _____ by car. (prefer)

4 Kate _____ e-mails. (prefer)

Maria _____ friends. (rather)

4 ★★ Write conversations using the cues.

1 (prefer / eat / hamburgers / hot dogs?)
(prefer / hot dogs)

A: *Would you prefer to eat hamburgers or hot dogs?*

B: *I'd prefer hot dogs.*

2 (rather / go shopping / watch a movie?)
(watch a movie)

A: _____

B: _____

3 (prefer / fly?)
(no / prefer / take the train)

A: _____

B: _____

4 (rather / take / English classes?)
(Yes / would)

A: _____

B: _____

5 (prefer / listen to / rap / rock music?)
(rap)

A: _____

B: _____

Use your English: Say good-bye

5 ★ Circle the correct words.

A Ceci: I'm going to Colombia tomorrow.

Louise: Oh, wow. 1 (Have)/ *Make* / *Take* a good trip.

Ceci: 2 I *do* / *will* / *have*.

***

B Neil: Mike and I are going surfing next week.

Rob: Well, 3 *be* / *have* / *take* care. Surfing is
dangerous.

Neil: Don't worry. We'll be OK.

Rob: Don't 4 *try* / *forget* / *stop* to text me.

Neil: I 5 *don't* / *haven't* / *won't*.

***

C Kerry: We're going to the U.K. next week.

Sean: Wow! That'll be great.

Kerry: I 6 *want* / *hope* / *wish* so.

Sean: 7 *Look* / *Take* / *See* you soon!

***

D Jack: Bye, Millie. Have a great vacation!

Millie: Thanks. You, 8 *same* / *too* / *like*.

Consolidation

6 Complete the conversation with the words and phrases from the box.

> • a wimp • I'd prefer • ~~I'd rather~~ • listen to
> • looks awesome • not to spend • than
> • to walk • up for it • you later

Nick: There's a concert at the youth club tonight. Do
you want to come?

Ron: No. 1 *I'd rather* stay at home and read a book.

Nick: Don't be such 2 _____ . Come on, come
to the club.

Ron: Which band is playing?

Nick: It's Jamie's band, The Redbridge Rappers. It's
their first concert.

Ron: Jamie? Oh, OK. I'm 3 _____ .
I'd rather 4 _____ rock music, but I like
Jamie. What time does it start?

Nick: At eight o'clock, but 5 _____ to get there
earlier. I want to see them and talk to Jamie
before the concert starts. I'm going to get
there at about six o'clock.

Ron: Six. OK. Do you want my dad to take you?

Nick: No, thanks. I'd prefer 6 _____ . Martha is
working in the coffee shop on Bridge Street.
I'll go in and say hello.

Ron: OK. See 7 _____ .

*** *6 P.M.* ***

Nick: Hi, Ron.

Ron: Hi, Nick. Wow! Jamie 8 _____ .
I like his hair!

Nick: Yes, it's great. Come on. Let's buy a soda or
something to drink.

Ron: No, thanks. I'd prefer 9 _____
any money tonight. I'd rather spend my
money on a movie 10 _____ on drinks.

Nick: Don't worry. I'll buy you a drink, and we can
watch your movie together next weekend.

Ron: Great idea! I'll have an orange juice, please.

INTEGRATED
CONSOLIDATION
SKILLS

Animal rights and wrongs

Before you read

1 Before you read, check the meaning of these words.

> **New words**
> • cage • cruel • silly • smells of
> • somewhere else • unnatural • vegetarian

Read

2 ★ Read Natalia's message and choose the correct summary of her problem.

1 Natalia doesn't like her cousins and wants to go to the zoo without them.

2 Natalia likes her cousins, but wants to meet her friends tomorrow and eat burgers.

3 Natalia likes her cousins, but she doesn't like the zoo or the coffee shop in the zoo.

4 Natalia's mom is going to take her and her cousins to the zoo tomorrow, and Natalia is very excited.

5 Natalia and her cousins want to go to the zoo tomorrow, but it is closed.

Hi, Carla,

1 _f_ I need some advice. My two young cousins are staying with us right now. 2 ___ They want to go to the zoo. They live in a small town, and they've never been to a zoo before. I really don't want to go to the zoo or any zoos! 3 ___ I think they're cruel and unnatural. My mom told me not to be so silly. She says our zoo is very nice, with big cages. 4 ___ My cousins are six and eight years old. They're nice boys, but I don't want to go to the zoo with them. If we go to the zoo coffee shop, they'll eat burgers. I know that coffee shop.

5 ___ There isn't any vegetarian food on the menu there, and it always smells of burgers.

What should I do? 6 ___ Should I tell my cousins that the zoo is closed? Should I take them somewhere else?

Write back or call me tonight, please!

Natalia

3 ★★ Read the message again and complete the blanks (2–6) in it with sentences (a–e).

a) She thinks the animals there are happy!

b) Should I lie?

c) I hate zoos.

d) I promised to take care of them tomorrow.

e) It's horrible.

f) I hope you're awake!

Listen

> **Learning strategy: Be a good listener!**
> **Remember!** While you listen, smile, nod your head, and say things like "OK," "Sure," "I see," "Really?"

4 ★ (14) Listen to Carla talking to Natalia. Circle the correct answers.

1 Carla is calling to (give) / *ask for* advice.

2 Carla says Natalia *should / shouldn't* lie.

3 Carla *knows / doesn't know* a good place to eat lunch.

4 Carla's advice is to write *an article about / a letter to* the zoo.

5 Natalia thinks Carla's advice is *bad / good*.

5 ★★ (14) Listen again. Complete Natalia's notes.

Advice from Carla:
Don't eat in the zoo coffee shop. Eat in the
1 Blue Dolphin coffee shop on 2 _____
Street. Good food - lots of 3 _____
meals. Take a 4 _____ , camera,
and a 5 _____ .
Look for problems in the zoo: small, dirty
6 _____ ; 7 _____ animals.

Write an article for website: www. 8 _____
A good article needs 9 _____ and
10 _____ , not just my opinions!
Carla is great!!

Write

6 ★ Look at the notes. On a piece of paper, write an e-mail from Melanie asking for advice and a reply from Ben giving advice.

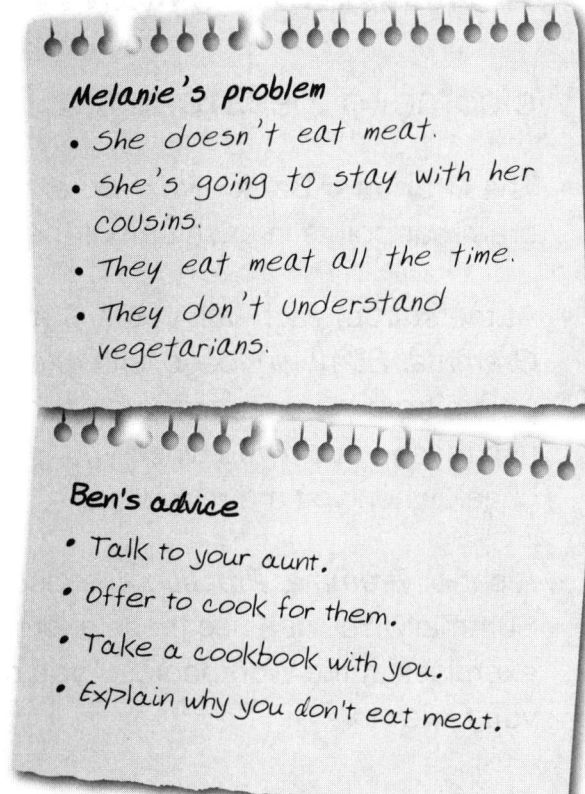

Melanie's problem
- *She doesn't eat meat.*
- *She's going to stay with her cousins.*
- *They eat meat all the time.*
- *They don't understand vegetarians.*

Ben's advice
- *Talk to your aunt.*
- *Offer to cook for them.*
- *Take a cookbook with you.*
- *Explain why you don't eat meat.*

Start Melanie's e-mail like this:

From:	Melanie
To:	Ben

Hi, Ben,
I have a problem and I need your advice. What should I do?

Start and end Ben's e-mail like this:

From:	Ben
To:	Melanie

Hi, Melanie,
Thanks for the e-mail. Why don't you . . .

Good luck! Have a nice time!
Ben

Grammar Bank

Welcome to the **Grammar Bank!**

- The **Grammar Bank** gives you extra practice for all the grammar points in each unit of the Student Book.

- At the start of each unit in the Grammar Bank, there is a *Grammar Summary* page with examples of all the grammar points from the unit and notes about grammar rules. You can use these to help you when you are doing an exercise and as a check when you are reviewing.

- A set of *Grammar Practice* exercises follows each Grammar Summary. You can use these exercises as a follow-up to the exercises in the Workbook, or you can use them later to help you review.

- At the end of each unit is a *Consolidation* exercise, which covers all the grammar points from the unit.

Grammar Summary

Simple present

Affirmative

I / You / We / You / They **live** in the U.S.
He / She **lives** in the U.S.
It **rains** a lot in the spring.

Negative

I / You / We / You / They **don't live** in Colombia.
He / She **doesn't live** in Colombia.
It **doesn't get** very cold here.

Questions

Do you **work** in a school?
Does he **work** in a school?
What do they **speak**?

Short answers

Yes, I **do**. / No, I **don't**.
Yes, he **does**. / No, he **doesn't**.
Spanish.

Adverbs and expressions of frequency

I **always** / **usually** / **often** / **sometimes** / **rarely** / **hardly ever** / **never** get up at seven o'clock.

You are **always** / **usually** / **often** / **sometimes** / **rarely** / **hardly ever** / **never** tired.

He gets home late **every day** / **once a week** / **twice a month** / **three times a year**.

Present continuous

Affirmative

I**'m watching** TV.
You / We / They**'re talking**.
He / She / **'s sleeping**.
It**'s getting** cold.

Negative

I**'m not playing** soccer.
You / We / They **aren't reading**.
He / She **isn't eating**.
It **isn't getting** warmer!

Questions

Am I **talking**?
Are you **shopping**?
Is she **reading**?
Are they **eating**?
What are they **eating**?

Short answers

Yes, you **are**. / No, you **aren't**.
Yes, I **am**. / No, I**'m not**.
Yes, she **is**. / No, she **isn't**.
Yes, they **are**. / No, they **aren't**.
Hamburgers.

Notes

Simple present

- For the third-person singular (*he*, *she*, *it*) affirmative, add *-s* to most verbs.
- In questions, the word order is: *Do* / *Does* + subject + infinitive (without *to*) + ?
- In short answers, do not repeat the main verb.
- Use the auxiliary *don't/doesn't* to make negatives.

Common mistakes

~~He get up at 6 A.M.~~ ✗
He gets up at 6 A.M. ✓
~~She doesn't likes swimming.~~ ✗
She doesn't like swimming. ✓
~~What time you go to school?~~ ✗
What time do you go to school? ✓

Adverbs and expressions of frequency

- Use these with the simple present to say how often we do something.
- Adverbs of frequency come after the verb *be*, but they come before other verbs.
- In negative sentences, they come between *don't/doesn't* and the verb.
- Put other expressions of frequency at the end of the sentence.

Present continuous

Form

- Use the verb *be* (*am/is/are*) + the base form of the main verb + *-ing* to form the affirmative.
- Add *-n't* (*not*) to the verb *be* to form negatives.
- In questions, the word order is: *Am/Is/Are* + subject + base form of main verb + *-ing*.

Common mistakes

~~They jogging.~~ ✗
They're jogging. ✓
~~You are watching TV?~~ ✗
Are you watching TV? ✓

Grammar Practice

Simple present

1 **Complete the sentences with the correct form of the verbs in parentheses.**

1 I *get up* (get up) early every day.

2 My sister _____ (like) TV.

3 My friend _____ (speak) Spanish.

4 You often _____ (listen) to music.

5 Max _____ (love) New York.

6 My parents _____ (work) in a hospital.

7 I _____ (live) in a big house.

8 Leon _____ (be) from Peru.

2 **Make the sentences negative.**

1 I live in Brazil.

   I don't live in Brazil.

2 My parents speak Portuguese.

   _____

3 My father works in a hospital.

   _____

4 Claudia likes rock music.

   _____

5 Natasha and Juan go to my school.

   _____

6 You sit next to me in class.

   _____

7 My dog eats fish.

   _____

3 **Write questions and short answers.**

1 you / like / Shakira? (✓)

   Do you like Shakira? *Yes, I do.*

2 Brad Pitt / speak / Chinese? (✗)

   _____

   _____

3 Venus and Serena Williams / come from / Canada? (✗)

   _____

   _____

4 Nani and Ronaldinho / speak / Portuguese? (✓)

   _____

   _____

5 Rafael Nadal / live / in Italy? (✗)

   _____

   _____

6 Le Bron James / play / basketball? (✓)

   _____

   _____

Adverbs and expressions of frequency

4 **Rewrite the sentences using the words in parentheses.**

1 My parents watch TV. (sometimes)

   My parents sometimes watch TV.

2 We skateboard. (never)

   _____

3 Sam has breakfast at home. (twice a week)

   _____

4 Tessa gets home early. (every day)

   _____

5 I read in bed. (hardly ever)

   _____

6 I play video games. (often)

   _____

7 Mel has a snack. (three times a day)

   _____

Present continuous

5 Complete the sentences using the present continuous.

1 I / watch / TV

I'm watching TV.

2 Dan / play / football

_____

3 your dad / have / a barbecue

_____

4 your parents / swim

_____

5 they / go / to the youth club

_____

6 your brother / surf / the net

_____

6 Write sentences using the cues.

1 I / listen to music ✗ / watch TV ✓

I'm not listening to music. I'm watching TV.

2 Julio and Dan / eat fast food ✗ / have a barbecue ✓

_____

_____

3 Chris / sleep ✗ / chat with his friends ✓

_____

_____

4 Maya and Elena / text ✗ / hang out with friends ✓

_____

_____

5 Louisa / play a video game ✗ / read ✓

_____

_____

7 Write questions and short answers about the people in Exercise 6.

1 I / watch TV?

Am I watching TV? Yes, I am.

2 Louisa / sleep?

Is Louisa sleeping? No, she isn't.

3 Julio and Dan / eating fast food?

_____

_____

4 Louisa / read?

_____

_____

5 Chris / chatting with his friends?

_____

_____

6 Maya and Elena / chatting online?

_____

_____

Consolidation

8 Complete the conversation with words from the box.

```
• are • Do • do • don't • every • have • like
• now • often • speaking • talk • writing
```

Lara: Hi, Soledad. Can I come in?

Soledad: Yes, of course.

Lara: Thanks. Are you doing anything right **1** *now*?

Soledad: I'm **2** _____ an e-mail to my parents.

Lara: Tell them that you're **3** _____ a lot of English. Your English is great!

Soledad: Thanks! You know, my after-school routine here is different than in Ecuador.

Lara: Really? What do you usually **4** _____ after school in Ecuador?

Soledad: I do my homework at three o'clock **5** _____ day, then I **6** _____ a snack at five o'clock. Then I'm free until I have dinner with my parents at eight o'clock.

Lara: **7** _____ you play video games?

Soledad: No, I **8** _____ . I don't **9** _____ video games or TV. I **10** _____ go out with my friends to a coffee shop. We sit and **11** _____ .

Lara: That's nice.

Soledad: So what **12** _____ you doing right now?

Lara: I'm doing my Spanish homework. Can you help me?

Soledad: Of course. No problem.

Grammar Summary

Simple present and present continuous

What **do you do** every day?
What **are you doing** right now?

I often **walk** to school.
I'm walking to school now.

He **doesn't usually watch** TV at night.
He **isn't watching** TV tonight.

whose . . . ?; Possessive 's and s'

Whose hat is this?
Whose pens are these?

Singular	Plural
It's Jack**'s** (car).	It's my parent**s'** (car).
They're John**'s** (CDs).	They're the student**s'** (CDs).
It's that woman**'s** coat.	They're the women**'s** coats.

Possessive adjectives and pronouns

It's **my** book.	It's **mine**.
They're **your** earrings.	They're **yours**.
It's **his** cell phone.	It's **his**.
They're **her** sunglasses.	They're **hers**.
They're **our** pens.	They're **ours**.
It's **their** car.	It's **theirs**.

Count and noncount nouns with *some*, *any*, and *no*

There's (is) **some** sugar.
There are **some** apples.

There isn't **any** salt. / There's (is) **no** salt.
There aren't **any** bananas. / There are **no** bananas.

Is there **any** pepper?
Are there **any** pears?

Notes

Simple present and present continuous

- Use the simple present to talk about daily habits, routines, and facts.
- Use the present continuous to talk about things happening right now.

whose . . . ?; Possessive 's and s'

Usage
- Use *'s/s'* to show possession.
- Use *whose* to ask about possession.

Form
- Add *'s* to all singular nouns and to plural nouns that do not end in -s.
- Add an apostrophe to regular plural nouns that end in -s.

Possessive adjectives and pronouns

- Use possessive adjectives with nouns.
- Use possessive pronouns in place of *my / your*, etc. + noun.

Common mistakes

Is this hers bag? ✗	*That's our.* ✗
Is this her bag? ✓	*That's ours.* ✓

Count and noncount nouns with *some*, *any*, and *no*

Usage
- Use *some* with plural count nouns and noncount nouns in affirmative sentences.
- Use *any* with plural count nouns, with noncount nouns in the negative, and in questions.
- Use *no* with singular and plural count and noncount nouns. *No* means *not one / not any*. We use *no* with an affirmative verb.

Form
- Count nouns can have a singular and plural form.
- Noncount nouns are not usually plural and only have one form.

Grammar Practice

Simple present and present continuous

1 Circle the correct phrases.

1 I *usually get up* / *am usually getting up* at seven o'clock.

2 You *don't often walk* / *aren't often walking* to school.

3 What *do you watch* / *are you watching* now?

4 How often *does Liz drive* / *is Liz driving* to work?

5 My mom *reads* / *'s reading* a magazine right now.

6 I can't go out now. I *do* / *'m doing* my homework.

7 *Do you ever go* / *Are you ever going* skiing in the winter?

8 *Does your sister listen* / *Is your sister listening* to music right now?

2 Write conversations using the cues.

1 A: What / you do / now?

B: I / surf the net

A: you / often / surf the net?

B: ✓

A: *What are you doing now?*

B: *I'm surfing the net.*

A: *Do you often surf the net?*

B: *Yes, I do.*

2 A: How often / your father / drive to Seattle?

B: He / drive / to Seattle / once a month

A: he / drive / there now?

B: ✗ / He / sleep

A: _____

B: _____

A: _____

B: _____

3 A: What / your mom / wear / right now?

B: She wear / her uniform.

A: she / always / wear / it at work?

B: ✓

A: _____

B: _____

A: _____

B: _____

whose . . . ?; Possessive *'s* and *s'*

3 Write sentences.

1 this bag / Mark

   This bag is Mark's.

2 that CD player / Nina

   _____

3 these sunglasses / Philippe

   _____

4 this book / Jorge

   _____

5 these pens / our teacher

   _____

6 this watch / my friend

   _____

7 this house / my parents

   _____

Possessives

4 Circle the correct words.

1 Is this *your* / *yours* bag?

2 That's *my* / *mine* bracelet.

3 Is that your *sister* / *sister's* hat?

4 My *parent's* / *parents'* skis are over there.

5 Where's *Carla'* / *Carla's* cell phone?

6 *Who* / *Whose* watch is this?

7 *Our* / *Ours* friends are very nice.

8 This is *your* / *yours* purse, and that is *her* / *hers*.

9 They're looking for *their* / *theirs* wallets.

10 Is this *Charles'* / *Charles's* towel?

Count and noncount nouns with *some*, *any*, and *no*

5 Write *C* for count nouns and *N* for noncount nouns.

What food is there?

1 *N*	salt ✓	5 ___	carrots ✓	9 ___	cheese ✓
2 ___	eggs ✗	6 ___	milk ✗	10 ___	tomatoes ✗
3 ___	sugar ✗	7 ___	nuts ✓		
4 ___	rice ✓	8 ___	lettuce ✗		

6 Write sentences about the list in Exercise 5 using *there is / are* and *there isn't / aren't*.

1 *There's some salt.*

2 *There aren't any eggs. / There are no eggs.*

3 _____

4 _____

5 _____

6 _____

7 _____

8 _____

9 _____

10 _____

7 Complete the second sentence so that it means the same as the first one.

1 Do we have any meat? *Is* there *any* meat?

2 There isn't any sugar. There's _____ sugar.

3 Do we have any tomatoes?

_____ there _____ tomatoes?

4 We have two melons. There _____ two melons.

5 There aren't any bananas. There _____ no bananas.

6 There's some rice. We _____ _____ rice.

7 We don't have any peas. There _____ any peas.

8 There's no salt. We _____ _____ _____ salt.

9 Do we have any milk? _____ _____ any milk?

10 We don't have any butter. There _____ _____ butter.

Consolidation

8 Circle the correct choices.

Dad: Alan. **1** (Are you doing) / *Do you do* anything right now?

Alan: Yes, I **2** *do / am*. I'm watching TV. Why?

Dad: I need some help. I **3** *cook / 'm cooking* dinner.

Alan: Really? You **4** *don't / aren't* usually cook dinner.

Dad: I know, but your mother's not feeling well.

Alan: Er . . . what's that?

Dad: It's beef.

Alan: We usually **5** *are having / have* chicken on Sundays. That's **6** *our / ours* favorite meal.

Dad: I know, but we don't have **7** *any / some* chicken, and I don't really know how to cook beef. There are **8** *any / no* ideas in this cookbook.

Alan: That's not **9** *Moms / Mom's*. That's Susie's. There **10** *aren't / isn't* any meat ideas in there. Susie doesn't eat meat.

Dad: Oh!

Alan: Here you are. Try this.

Grammar Summary

Verbs of emotion + gerund form (*-ing*)

I **love playing** football.
She/He **likes watching** TV.
We **don't mind walking** to school.
I **don't like doing** gymnastics.
You **hate being** late.
They **enjoy cooking**.
She/He **prefers swimming** (to playing tennis).

Imperatives

Affirmative	Negative
Come here!	**Don't do** that!
Sit down!	**Don't talk** in here.

must/must not for rules

Affirmative	Negative
I **must do** this work.	We **must not eat** in class.
We **must work** hard.	You **must not wear** shoes in here.
They **must be** careful.	They **must not play** in here.

be going to for future plans, intentions, and, predictions

Affirmative	Negative
I'm going to watch TV tonight.	**I'm not going to go** to the party.
You're going to go out.	You **aren't going to stay** home.
He's going to have fish for dinner.	He **isn't going to have** chicken.
She**'s going to play** tennis later.	She **isn't going to play** basketball.
We**'re going to have** a test soon.	We **aren't going to do** a project.
They**'re going to study** French.	They **aren't going to study** Spanish.

Questions	Short answers
Are you **going to play** tennis?	Yes, I **am**. / No, I'm **not**.
Is John **going to cook** dinner?	Yes, he **is**. / No, he **isn't**.
Are they **going to go** swimming?	Yes, they **are**. / No, they **aren't**.

Notes

Verbs of emotion + gerund form (*-ing*)

- Use the gerund form (*-ing*) after certain verbs of emotion (*like, love, hate*, etc.).
- Use the base form of a verb + *-ing* to form a gerund.

Common mistakes
I like play football. ✗
He hates listen to rock music. ✗

Imperatives

Usage
- We often use *please* with the imperative to be more polite.

Form
- To form affirmative imperatives, use the base form of the verb.
- To form negative imperatives, add *don't* before the base form of the verb.

must/must not for rules

Usage
- Use *must/must not* to say when it is necessary for someone to do or not to do something.

Form
- Use *must/must not* + the base form of a verb.

Common mistakes
I must to go home now. ✗
You mustn't talking. ✗

be going to for future plans, intentions, and predictions

Usage
- Use *be going to* to talk about plans and intentions for the future or to make predictions about a present situation.
- Use future time phrases to talk about the future with *be going to*.

Form
- Use *be going to* + the base form of a verb.

Common mistakes
I going to save my money this year. ✗
We not going to have a party on Friday. ✗

3 Grammar Practice

Verbs of emotion + gerund form (-ing)

1 Read Mike's profile and complete the sentences.

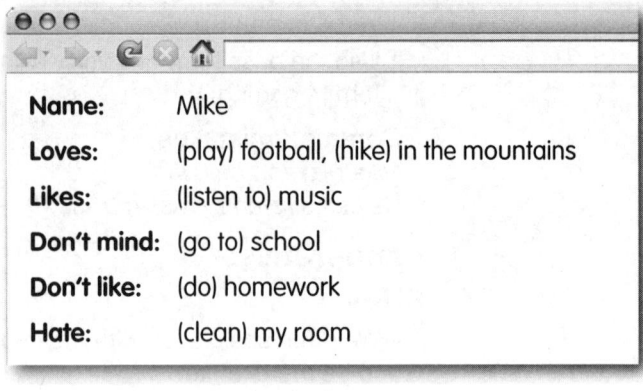

Name:	Mike
Loves:	(play) football, (hike) in the mountains
Likes:	(listen to) music
Don't mind:	(go to) school
Don't like:	(do) homework
Hate:	(clean) my room

1 *He loves playing* football.

2 _____ in the mountains.

3 _____ to school.

4 _____ to music.

5 _____ his room.

6 _____ homework.

2 Complete the questions using the correct form of verbs from the box.

> • do • go • ~~listen to~~ • watch

1 *Does* your father like *listening to* rock music?

2 _____ your parents like _____ on vacation?

3 _____ your mom enjoy _____ ice skating on TV?

4 _____ your friends hate _____ their homework?

3 Write questions for the answers.

1 A: Where *do you like going* on vacation?

B: I like going to the beach on vacation.

2 A: Who _____ at school?

B: I like sitting next to my friend Tomás at school.

3 A: What kind _____ to?

B: My friends like listening to rap music.

4 A: What _____ on Friday nights?

B: I enjoy going to the movies.

Imperatives

4 Complete the signs with the imperative form of the verbs from the box.

> • eat • ~~pay~~ • run • sit • ~~swim~~
> • talk • use • wait

Tickets $10
pay here

①

Don't swim here.

②

_____ in the school

③

PLEASE

_____ down and _____ for the doctor.

④

_____ in this room.

⑤

Test rules:
_____ a pen.
_____ to your friends. You must be quiet! Put your bags on the floor—not on the desk.

⑥

must/must not for rules

5 Look at the House Rules blog on page 107 and write what the person must and must not do.

1 *I must do my homework before I watch TV.*

2 *I must not watch more than two hours of TV a night.*

3 _____

4 _____

5 _____

6 _____

7 _____

8 _____

House rules

These are things my parents say I must and must not do.
What do you think about them?

1 Do my homework before I watch TV. (✓)
2 Watch more than two hours of TV a night. (✗)
3 Eat dinner with my family. (✓)
4 Be home before 11 P.M. on the weekend. (✓)
5 Be late for school. (✗)
6 Eat in my room. (✗)
7 Clean my room once a week. (✓)
8 Shout at my sister. (✗)

be going to for future plans, intentions, and predictions

6 Look at the flier and correct the information in Matthew's e-mail.

School sports day

Melanie – the broad jump   Jack and Mike – judo
Kate – gymnastics   Sean – swimming
Angie and Phil – karate   Ernesto – run

To: Ben

Dear Ben,
Here is the list of who's doing what on sports day.
Melanie is going to do judo, Kate is going to play
tennis, Angie and Phil are going to swim, Jack
and Mike are going to do karate, Sean is going to
do gymnastics, and you're going to ride a bike.
See you soon,
Matthew

To: Matthew

Dear Matthew,
Thanks for the e-mail. There are a few mistakes in it.

1 Melanie *isn't going to do judo. She's going to do the broad jump* .
2 Kate _____ .
3 Angie and Phil _____ .
4 Jack and Mike _____ .
5 Sean _____ .
6 I _____ .

Ernesto

7 Write questions and short answers about the sports day in Exercise 6.

1 Melanie / do karate?
   A: *Is Melanie going to do karate?*
   B: *No, she isn't.*
2 Ernesto / run?
   A: _____
   B: _____
3 Kate / do gymnastics?
   A: _____
   B: _____
4 Angie and Phil / play tennis?
   A: _____
   B: _____
5 Jack and Mike / do judo?
   A: _____
   B: _____

Consolidation

8 Complete the conversations with the correct form of the verbs given.

1 go

Simon: Do you want to go out tonight?
Umberto: Yes, OK. I don't mind *going* out.
          Where should we go?
Simon: Well, I know that Ed and Emily _____
          _____ to the movies.
Umberto: Oh, no! I hate _____ out with them.
          How about _____ somewhere else?

2 do

Juanita: What _____ you _____ at the
          school sports day next week, Beth?
Beth: I _____ anything!
Juanita: But you love _____ gymnastics.
Beth: I know, but I have a bad knee. The doctor
          said I must not _____ any sports
          for two months.
Juanita: Oh, that's terrible!
Beth: I don't mind _____ nothing. I can
          watch the others and cheer them on.

Grammar Summary

Comparative and superlative forms of adjectives

Our house is **older than** your house.
This room is **bigger than** our room.
This bag is **heavier than** that bag.
This chair is **more comfortable than** that chair.
Yards are **better than** balconies.
Regular sodas are **worse than** diet sodas.
My house is **farther** from school **than** your house.

This is **the smallest** room in the house.
July is **the hottest** month of the year.
Those are **the prettiest** flowers in the garden.
Lima is **the most important** city in Peru.
Mr. Smith is **the best** teacher in our school.
I'm **the worst** tennis player in my class.
Which hotel is **the farthest** from downtown?

Count and noncount nouns with *much, many, a lot of, a few, a little*

Affirmative
There are **a lot of** people here.
There's **a lot of** traffic on the roads.
There are **a few** tomatoes in the refrigerator.
There's **a little** milk in there, too.

Negative
There aren't **many** books.
There isn't **much** money.

Questions
How **many** potatoes are there?
How **much** luggage is there?

Question word *how* + adjectives of dimension

How tall / wide / long / high is it?
It's . . . **tall / wide / long / high**.

How heavy is it? / **How much** does it **weigh**?
It **weighs** . . .

How far is it?
It's . . . (from here / away).

Notes

Comparative and superlative forms of adjectives

Usage
• Use comparatives to compare two people or things.
• Use superlatives to compare a person or a thing with two or more people or things.

Irregular forms
• *good – better – the best*
  bad – worse – the worst
  far – farther – the farthest

Spelling rules
• To form a comparative, we add *-er* to the adjective.
• To form a superlative, we add *-est*.
• For adjectives ending in *-e*, drop the final *e* and add *-er* or *-est*.
• For adjectives ending in *-y*, change *-y* to *-i*.
• For adjectives ending in one vowel + one consonant, we usually double the final consonant.
• For long adjectives, use *more/most*.

Count and noncount nouns with *much, many, a lot of, a few, a little*
• Use *a lot of* with plural count nouns and with noncount nouns in affirmative sentences.
• Use *a few* and *a little* in affirmative sentences. Use *a few* with count nouns and *a little* with noncount nouns.
• Use *many* with plural count nouns and *much* with noncount nouns in negative statements and in questions.

Question word *how* + adjectives of dimension
• Use *how* + an adjective of dimension to ask questions about distances, heights, weights, etc.

Grammar Practice

Comparative and superlative forms of adjectives

1 Look at the hotel information and write sentences using comparative adjectives.

	Belle Vue	Rest House	Travel Stop
Built	1986	1974	1998
Price per night	$160	$140	$100
Rooms	100	40	60
Rating	★★★★	★★★★★	★★★

1 Belle Vue / Rest House (modern)
The Belle Vue is more modern than the Rest House.

2 Belle Vue / Travel Stop (old)

_____

3 Rest House / Travel Stop (expensive)

_____

4 Travel Stop / Belle Vue (cheap)

_____

5 Travel Stop / Rest House (big)

_____

6 Rest House / Belle Vue (small)

_____

7 Belle Vue / Travel Stop (good)

_____

8 Travel Stop / Rest House (bad)

_____

2 Use superlative adjectives in sentences about the hotels in Exercise 1.

1 (cheap) *The Travel Stop is the cheapest hotel.*

2 (old) _____

3 (good) _____

4 (expensive) _____

5 (bad) _____

6 (big) _____

7 (modern) _____

8 (small) _____

Count and noncount nouns with *much, many, a lot of, a few, a little*

3 Correct the mistakes.

         is   little
1 There ~~are~~ a ~~few~~ space.

2 I don't have much eggs.

3 Is there many music?

4 I have a little exercises to do for homework.

5 There aren't much traffic.

6 Do you have much bags?

4 Complete the paragraph with the correct quantity words from the box.

> • a few • a little • a little • ~~a lot of~~
> • a lot of • many • many • much
> • much • much

I spend **1** *a lot of* money on CDs—about $30 a month. I only get an allowance of $10 a week, so I don't have **2** _____ money for other things. I sometimes buy **3** _____ candy, but not **4** _____ because it isn't healthy. At the end of the week, I usually have **5** _____ money for a cup of coffee with my friends. My friends and I meet in a coffee shop downtown. There aren't **6** _____ good places to meet, and there isn't **7** _____ to do. I prefer spending my money on CDs. I don't have **8** _____ friends—just one or two—but they're real friends. Some people have **9** _____ "friends"—20 or 30—but when they have problems, only **10** _____ of these "friends" want to help them.

Question word *how* + adjectives of dimension

5 Look at the fact file. Complete the questions.

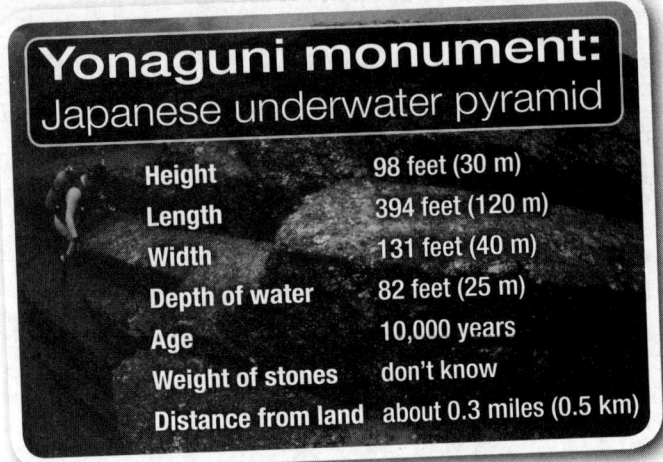

Yonaguni monument:
Japanese underwater pyramid

Height	98 feet (30 m)
Length	394 feet (120 m)
Width	131 feet (40 m)
Depth of water	82 feet (25 m)
Age	10,000 years
Weight of stones	don't know
Distance from land	about 0.3 miles (0.5 km)

1 *How long is the* Yonaguni monument?—394 feet.

2 _____ water?—82 feet.

3 _____ the monument?—98 feet.

4 _____ the monument?—131 feet.

5 _____ the stones?—We don't know.

6 _____ the stones weigh?—We don't know.

7 _____ the monument from land?
 —About 0.3 miles

6 Use the numbers to complete the sentences about the Yonaguni monument in Exercise 5.

1 10,000

 The monument is ten thousand years old .

2 98

 The monument _____ .

3 394

 The monument _____ .

4 131

 The monument _____ .

5 82

 The water _____ .

6 0.3

 The monument _____ .

Consolidation

7 Complete the conversation with words from the box.

> • few • farther • height • How • ~~lot~~
> • more • more • most • much • taller
> • than • the

Carlos: What do you have there?

Juan: It's a book of interesting facts.

Carlos: Are there a **1** *lot* of facts in it?

Juan: Hundreds.

Carlos: Tell me some.

Juan: I don't have **2** _____ time.

Carlos: OK, just one.

Juan: OK. The **3** _____ popular tourist destination in the U.S. is Disney World in Florida, with 16 million visitors a year.

Carlos: Why is Disney World **4** _____ popular **5** _____ other places, like the Grand Canyon?

Juan: Well, it's **6** _____ exciting than the Grand Canyon, and the Grand Canyon is **7** _____ from most big cities. I have to go. I only have a **8** _____ minutes before my English class starts.

Carlos: One more fact.

Juan: OK. The Burj Khalifa is **9** _____ tallest building in the world.

Carlos: **10** _____ tall is it?

Juan: Its **11** _____ is 2,716 feet, or 828 meters. Wow. That's almost 1,000 feet **12** _____ than the Willis Tower in Chicago. . . . Oh, no! Look at the time!

Carlos: So, does your book say what the fastest time to get from here to an English class is?

Juan: No, it doesn't, but it's going to be 38 seconds! That's how quick I'm going to be!

5 Grammar Summary

Simple past of the verb *be*

Affirmative
I / He / She **was** at home last night.
It **was** cold yesterday.
You / We / They **were** born in 1995.

Negative
I / He / She **wasn't** at school.
It **wasn't** hot yesterday.
You / We / They **weren't** born in 1994.

Questions
Were you at home yesterday?
Was I right?
Was he late?
Were you good students?
Were they at the party?

Short answers
Yes, I **was**. / No, I **wasn't**.
Yes, you **were**. / No, you **weren't**.
Yes, he **was**. / No, he **wasn't**.
Yes, we **were**. / No, we **weren't**.
Yes, they **were**. / No, they **weren't**.

Past adverbial phrases

I was at school **last night / last week / last month / last year**.
He was here **on Monday / on the weekend / in July / in 1994**.

Simple past of regular verbs

Affirmative
I / You / He / She / We / They **watched** TV last night.

Negative
I / You / He / She / We / They **didn't watch** TV last night.

Questions
Did I / you / he / she / we / they **watch** TV last night?

Short answers
Yes, I / you / he / she / we / they **did**.
No, I / you / he / she / we / they **didn't**.

Simple past of irregular verbs

Affirmative
I / You / He / She / We / They **went** to the movies last week.

Negative
I / You / He / She / We / They **didn't go** to the movies last week.

Questions
Did I / you / he / she / we / they **go** to the movies last week?

Short answers
Yes, I / you / he / she / we / they **did**.
No, I / you / he / she / we / they **didn't**.

Past adverbial phrases with *ago*

I left school **a week ago**.

Notes

Simple past of the verb *be*

Usage
- Use the simple past of *be* to talk about the past.

Form
- To form negatives, use *was/were* + *not* (*n't*).
- For questions, use this word order: *be* + subject.

Common mistakes
We was at a party. ✗
We were at a party. ✓

Simple past

Usage
- Use the simple past for actions and situations that started and finished in the past.

Form
- To form the simple past of most regular verbs, add *-ed* to the verb.
- To form negatives, use *didn't* + the base form of the verb.
- To form questions, use *Did* + subject + the base form of the verb.
- When a verb ends in *-e*, add *-d*.
- When a verb ends in a consonant + *-y*, change *-y* to *-i* and then add *-ed*.
- When a verb ends in one vowel + consonant, double the final consonant.
- Go to www.pearsonlongman.com/insync for a list of irregular past forms.

Common mistakes
Did you went to a party? ✗
Did you go to a party? ✓

Past adverbial phrases

When we talk about past events, we often use past time expressions to tell when an event happened.

Past adverbial phrases with *ago*

- Use *ago* with a past time expression, or adverbial phrase, to talk about when a past event happened.

Simple past of the verb *be*

1 **Complete the sentences with *was* or *were*.**

1 I *was* on vacation last week.

2 You _____ 15 last July.

3 Sergio and Manuel _____ late for school yesterday.

4 Julio _____ with me at the movies last night.

5 My dad _____ at work until 11 P.M. yesterday.

6 My cousins _____ born in Mexico.

7 This town _____ very important 200 years ago.

8 My friends and I _____ on TV last week.

2 **Look at the information in the boxes and correct the sentences.**

Last week

My brother: at school   The game: awful

My parents: at work   My sister: on vacation

My friends: on a school trip

1 Last week, my brother was on vacation.

He wasn't on vacation. He was at school.

2 The game last week was great.

_____

3 My parents were at home last week.

_____

4 My sister was at school last week.

_____

5 My friends were on vacation last week.

_____

Last summer

The hotel: small   The burgers: horrible

The weather: great   The sea: cold

My parents: relaxed

6 The hotel we stayed in last summer was big.

_____

7 The burgers we ate on vacation were delicious.

_____

8 The weather last summer was terrible.

_____

9 The sea on vacation was very warm.

_____

10 My parents were worried on our vacation.

_____

3 **Read the answers. Complete the questions.**

1 When *were you* born?

I was born in 1994.

2 Where _____ night?

My parents were at a restaurant last night.

3 Who _____ school?

Steve Cobb was my best friend in elementary school.

4 What _____ in 2010?

My favorite movie in 2010 was *Iron Man 2*.

5 How many _____ party?

There were about 50 people at the party.

6 Where _____ yesterday?

Beth was at home at 10 P.M. yesterday.

7 Who _____ morning?

My sister was in the bathroom at eight o'clock this morning.

8 Where _____ Cup?

The 2010 World Cup was in South Africa.

Simple past of regular verbs

4 **Complete the sentences with the appropriate affirmative or negative form of the verb.**

1 I liked the chicken at the restaurant, but I _didn't like_ the salad.

2 I _____ a movie last night, but I didn't watch a soap opera.

3 Ben _____ for a shirt at the mall on Saturday, but he didn't look for any shoes.

4 My brother walked to school yesterday, but he _____ home again.

5 I _____ my phone, but I didn't drop my camera.

6 We listened to a Miley Cyrus CD, but we _____ to a Taylor Swift CD.

7 They ordered a pizza for lunch, but they _____ any french fries.

8 I _____ my mom's birthday, but I didn't remember my dad's birthday.

9 I talked to my friend on the phone last weekend, but I _____ to my sister.

10 I _____ to my e-mails last night, but I didn't reply to my text messages.

5 **Write questions and answers.**

1 What movie / you watch / last night? (a comedy)
What movie did you watch last night?
I watched a comedy.

2 What food / your parents need / yesterday? (fruit)
_____
_____

3 Who / you call / this morning? (my cousin)
_____
_____

4 Who / you text / this morning? (Maria)
_____
_____

5 What / your parents listen to / last night? (some jazz CDs)
_____
_____

6 How many suitcases / they pack / last night? (three)
_____
_____

Simple past of irregular verbs

6 **Complete the table with the correct infinitives or past forms.**

infinitives	past forms
go	1 _went_
2 _____	bought
fall	3 _____
think	4 _____
5 _____	said
come	6 _____
do	7 _____
8 _____	told
see	9 _____
have	10 _____
11 _____	took
lose	12 _____

7 **Complete the paragraph with the simple past forms of the verbs in the box.**

> • buy • get up • give • go • have • leave
> • lose • make • say • take • write

Yesterday, I **1** _got up_ at 9:30, and I **2** _____ a shower. Then Mom **3** _____ breakfast for me. After that, she **4** _____ , "We need food from the supermarket. Can you go shopping for me?" She **5** _____ down the things we needed on a shopping list. So I **6** _____ to the supermarket. I **7** _____ all the things on mom's list, and then I **8** _____ the store. Suddenly, someone yelled, "Excuse me!" It was a cute girl! She said, **9** " _____ you _____ your cell phone? I just found this one." She **10** _____ my phone! I thanked her. Then we talked for a while, and guess what? She **11** _____ me her phone number!

8 Complete the conversations with the correct form of the verbs provided.

1 wear

Sara: What **1** _do_ you usually _wear_ ?

Lina: I usually **2** _____ jeans and a T-shirt, but yesterday I **3** _____ jeans because it was graduation day.

Sara: What **4** _____ you _____ ?

Lina: I **5** _____ a nice dress.

2 go

Mick: Where **6** _____ you usually _____ on vacation?

Juan: We usually **7** _____ to Mexico or Peru.

Mick: **8** _____ you _____ there last year?

Juan: We **9** _____ to Guadalajara in Mexico, but we **10** _____ to Peru.

Past adverbial phrases

9 Circle the correct time expressions.

1 What time did you get up (yesterday) / last morning?

2 I saw Joe yesterday / last week in the park.

3 Did you study hard yesterday / last night?

4 I can't believe that our vacation in Brazil was just last year / next summer.

5 We found a great new fast-food restaurant yesterday / tomorrow.

6 What time did you get home yesterday / last night?

Past adverbial phrases with *ago*

10 Write sentences with *ago* using the cues.

1 Today: July 12 / *Twilight: Eclipse* / July 7 (see)

I saw "Twilight: Eclipse" five days ago.

2 Now: 2 P.M. / Stefan / 11 A.M. (arrive)

_____

3 Now: August / my parents / new car / June (buy)

_____

_____

4 Today: Monday / accident / Thursday (happen)

_____

_____

5 Now: January / I / July (graduate)

_____

_____

Consolidation

11 Complete the conversation with the correct past form of the verbs in parentheses.

Mom: How **1** _was_ (be) the movie last night?

Joe: It **2** _____ (be) great, thanks.

Mom: That's good, but you **3** _____ (be) back late. What **4** _____ (happen)?

Joe: I'm sorry. I **5** _____ (miss) the last bus.

Mom: Why?

Joe: The movie **6** _____ (not end) until 10:30. I **7** _____ (want) to get a taxi. There **8** _____ (not be) any taxis, so I waited. A taxi **9** _____ (come) after 20 minutes, but I realized that I **10** _____ (not have) enough money for it.

Mom: **11** _____ you _____ (walk) all the way home?

Joe: Yes, I **12** _____ (do). It wasn't much fun!

6 Grammar Summary

Past continuous

Affirmative
I **was working**.
You **were talking**.
He **was sleeping**.
She **was shopping**.
It **was raining**.
We **were dancing**.
They **were eating** burgers.

Negative
I **wasn't sleeping**.
You **weren't reading**.
He **wasn't watching** TV.
She **wasn't texting** her friend.
It **wasn't snowing**.
We **weren't singing**.
They **weren't drinking** coffee.

Questions
Was I **sleeping**?
Were you **dancing** yesterday?
Was he **shouting**?
Was she **crying**?
Was it **raining**?
Were you playing **tennis**?
Were we **dancing** then?
Were they **skiing**?

Short answers
Yes, you **were**. / No, you **weren't**.
Yes, I **was**. / No, I **wasn't**.
Yes, he **was**. / No, he **wasn't**.
Yes, she **was**. / No, she **wasn't**.
Yes, it **was**. / No, it **wasn't**.
Yes, we **were**. / No, we **weren't**.
Yes, we **were**. / No, we **weren't**.
Yes, they **were**. / No, they **weren't**.

Past continuous and simple past with *while* and *when*

While I **was watching** TV, the phone **rang**.
The phone **rang while** I **was watching** TV.

I **was watching** TV **when** the phone **rang**.
When the phone **rang**, I **was watching** TV.

Adjective clauses with *who, that,* and *where*

They are the people **who** e-mailed us.
I want to see a movie **that** makes me laugh.
This is the town **where** I was born.

Notes

Past continuous

Usage
• Use the past continuous to talk about something that was happening or was in progress at a certain time in the past.

Form
• To form the past continuous, use the past form of *be + -ing*.

Past continuous and simple past with *while* and *when*

• Use the simple past and the past continuous together to talk about an action that happened at the same time as another action. Use the past continuous for the longer action that was in progress. Use the simple past for the shorter, finished action.
• Use *while* before the past continuous.
• Use *when* before the simple past.
• When we use *when* or *while* at the beginning of a sentence, we link the two parts of the sentence with a comma.

Common mistakes
When I was watching TV, my friend called. ✗
While I was watching TV, my friend called. ✓
I was walking home while I saw my friends. ✗
I was walking home when I saw my friends. ✓

Adjective clauses with *who, that,* and *where*

• Use adjective clauses to describe or give information about a person or thing.
• Use *who* to talk about people.
• Use *that* to talk about things.
• Use *where* to talk about places.

Common mistakes
He's the boy which took my sandwiches. ✗
He's the boy who took my sandwiches. ✓
It's a place where I love. ✗
It's a place that I love. ✓

Past continuous

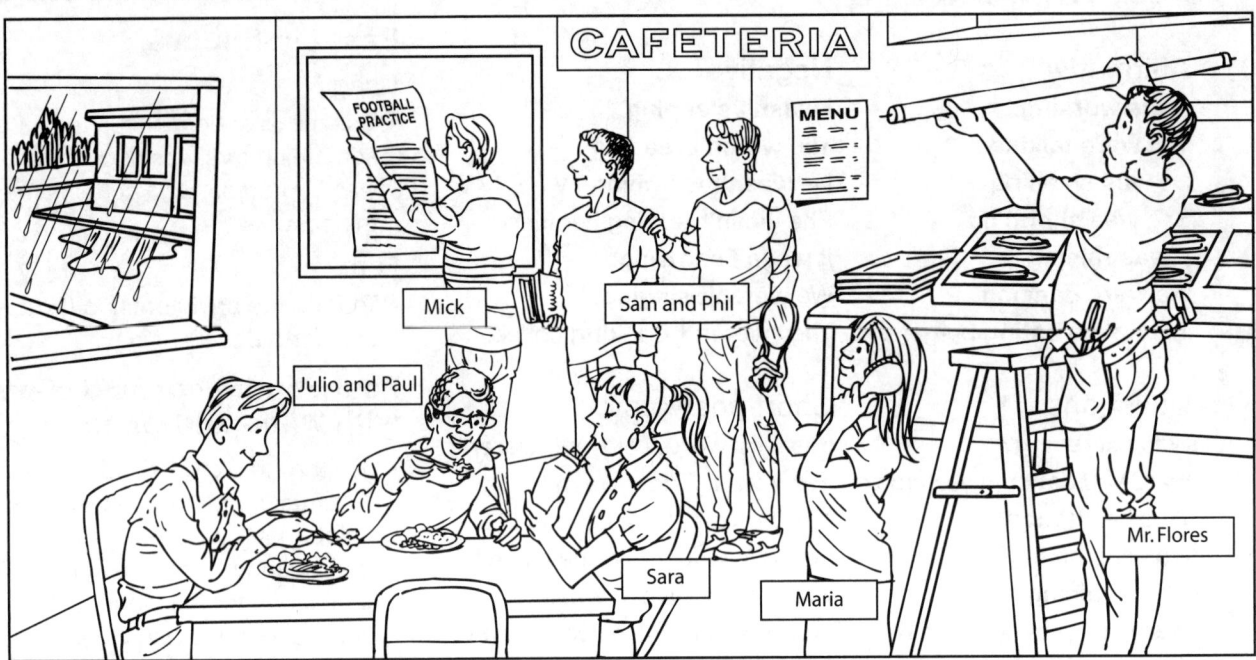

1 **Look at the picture and write sentences using the cues.**

At lunch yesterday, . . .

1 Julio and Paul / eat / their school lunches

Julio and Paul were eating their school lunches.

2 Sara / drink / orange juice

_____

_____

3 Mick / put / a sign on the board

_____

_____

4 Sam and Phil / read / the sign

_____

_____

5 Mr. Flores / stand / on a ladder

_____

_____

6 it / rain / outside

_____

_____

2 **Look at the picture again and correct the sentences.**

At lunch yesterday, . . .

1 Julio and Paul were eating sandwiches.

They weren't eating sandwiches. They were eating school lunches.

2 Maria was brushing her teeth.

_____

_____

3 Sara was standing up.

_____

_____

4 Sam and Phil were drawing on Mick's sign.

_____

_____

5 Mr. Flores was looking at the clock.

_____

_____

6 The sun was shining outside.

_____

_____

3 Write questions about the picture on p. 116.

1 What _were Julio and Paul eating?_

They were eating their school lunches.

2 What _____?

She was drinking orange juice.

3 What _____?

She was holding a brush and a mirror.

4 Where _____ the sign?

He was putting it on the bulletin board.

5 How many _____ the sign?

Two people were reading the sign.

6 What _____ on?

He was standing on a ladder.

4 Use the words to write questions and then write short answers.

1 Julio and Paul / eat sandwiches?

Were Julio and Paul eating sandwiches?

No, they weren't.

2 Sara / drink orange juice?

_____

_____

3 Maria / cut her hair?

_____

_____

4 Mick / put a sign on the board?

_____

_____

5 Sam and Phil / read the sign?

_____

_____

6 Mr. Flores / stand on a desk?

_____

_____

7 Mr. Flores / look at the light?

_____

_____

8 it rain?

_____

_____

Past continuous and simple past with *while* and *when*

5 Circle the correct form of the verb (simple past or past continuous).

1 When we (left) / were leaving the coffee shop, it rained / (was raining).

2 While we waited / were waiting for a bus, my dad arrived / was arriving.

3 They watched / were watching a movie when their aunt called / was calling.

4 Mark talked / was talking when the test started / was starting.

5 We didn't listen / weren't listening to any music while my dad slept / was sleeping.

6 We didn't do / weren't doing anything when the police stopped / were stopping us.

6 Write sentences using the cues.

1 we were waiting for the bus / we saw a fire (while)

While we were waiting for the bus, we saw a fire.

2 he was swimming / someone stole his wallet (when)

He was swimming when someone stole his wallet.

3 we were sitting in the yard / a ball came over the fence (while) _____

_____

4 the train was leaving / I arrived at the station (when)

_____

5 I was downloading music / my computer crashed (while) _____

6 she was skiing fast / she hit a tree (when)

_____

Adjective clauses with *who*, *that*, and *where*

7 Write the words in the correct order to describe the people, things, and places from the movies.

1 *Harry Potter*

a / He's / do / boy / can / magic / who

He's a boy who can do magic.

2 *Transformers*

are / are from / that / They / robots / another planet

_____

3 *Narnia*

place / a / live / where / It's / magical creatures

_____

4 *Tintin*

young journalist / He's / who / a / has / adventures / exciting

_____

5 *Cats & Dogs*

animals / They / that / fight / are / with each other

_____

8 Match the beginnings (1–8) to the endings (a–h). Then complete the sentences using *who*, *that*, or *where*.

1 A doctor is a person *g*
2 A school is a place ___
3 A theater is a building ___
4 The hero has a key ___
5 Krypton is the planet ___

a) you can watch movies.
b) opens a secret door.
c) sells great T-shirts.
d) also takes photos.
e) gives us the most homework.

6 Mr. Davies is the teacher ___
7 This is the store ___
8 This is a phone ___

f) students learn.
g) works in a hospital.
h) Superman was born.

1 A doctor is a person *who works in a hospital* .
2 A school is a place _____ .
3 A theater is a building _____ .
4 The hero has a key _____ .
5 Krypton is the planet _____ .
6 Mr. Davies is the teacher _____ .
7 This is the store _____ .
8 This is a phone _____ .

Consolidation

9 Write conversations using the cues.

1 Sam: I / jog / yesterday when / meet Phil
  Ryan: Who?
  Sam: You know. The boy / know a lot about computers

  Sam: *I was jogging yesterday when I met Phil.*

  Ryan: Who?

  Sam: You know. *The boy who knows a lot about computers.*

2 Kelly: I / watch / TV yesterday / when / Jack / call
  Mia: Who?
  Kelly: You know. The boy / live next door.

  Kelly: _____
  _____

  Mia: Who?
  Kelly: You know. _____
  _____

3 Juan: While / I / listen to the radio yesterday / I hear / a song by that singer
  Dan: Which singer?
  Juan: The one / played a concert here last month. He has long, dark hair.

  Juan: _____
  _____

  Dan: Which singer?
  Juan: _____ .
  _____

  He has long, dark hair.

Grammar Summary

too + adjective (+ infinitive)

Their house is **too far** from here **to walk**.
The water is **too cold to swim** in.
The homework took **too long to finish**.

(not) + adjective + enough (+ infinitive)

This house **is big enough to hold** most of our things.
This house **isn't big enough to hold** all of our things.
This house **isn't big enough to have** a party.

Present continuous for future plans

Affirmative

I'm meeting her tomorrow.
You're having a party next week.
He's seeing the doctor later.
She's going out tonight.
It's starting in an hour.
We're taking a test at ten o'clock.
They're playing tennis at 2 P.M.

Negative

I'm not meeting her tomorrow.
You aren't having a party next week.
He isn't seeing the doctor later.
She isn't going out tonight.
It isn't starting in an hour.
We aren't taking a test at ten o'clock.
They aren't playing tennis at 2 P.M.

Questions

Are you working tonight?
Am I meeting you tomorrow?
Is he swimming later?
Is it starting soon?
Is she going to the movies today?
Are we having a party on Sunday?
Are they eating out this evening?

Short answers

Yes, **I am.** / No, **I'm not.**
Yes, **you are.** / No, **you aren't.**
Yes, **he is.** / No, **he isn't.**
Yes, **it is.** / No, **it isn't.**
Yes, **she is.** / No, **she isn't.**
Yes, **we are.** / No, **we aren't.**
Yes, **they are.** / No, **they aren't.**

like and would like

I like eating fast food.
He doesn't like watching TV.
Do you like playing soccer?

I'd like to eat pizza tonight.
Would you like to play soccer later?

Notes

too + adjective (+ infinitive); (not) + adjective + enough (+ infinitive)

- *too* + adjective means there is more than we need/want.
- *not* + adjective + *enough* means there is less than we need/want.

Common mistake
The road isn't enough wide. ✗
The road isn't wide enough. ✓

Present continuous for future plans

- Use the present continuous to talk about future plans.
- Sometimes you can use either the present continuous or *be going to*.
- The more definite the plan, the more natural it is to use the present continuous instead of *be going to*.

like and would like

Usage
- Use *like* (+ verb + *-ing*) to talk about things we always like.
- Use *would like* (+ *to* + infinitive) to talk about preferences at a given time.
- Use *would like* + *to* + infinitive/noun to offer something to somebody or to invite someone to do something.

Form
- The short form of *would* is *'d*.
- To form negatives, add *n't* (*not*) to *would*.
- To form questions, use this word order: *Would* + subject.

Common mistake
You like to eat now? ✗
Would you like to eat now? ✓

too + adjective (+ infinitive); (not) + adjective + enough (+ infinitive)

1 Circle the correct words.

1 It's (too hot) / not hot enough.

2 It 's too quiet / isn't quiet enough.

3 It's too big / not big enough.

4 The test was not difficult enough / too difficult.

5 She has too much / enough money.

6 There's too much / not enough traffic.

2 Write sentences using the words in parentheses.

1 I can't swim in the swimming pool. (it / cold)

It's too cold.

2 You can't go for a walk in the forest. (it / dangerous)

_____

3 They don't want to eat in this restaurant. (it / dirty)

_____

4 She can't wear these shoes. (they / small)

_____

5 I can't afford to take my family to that zoo. (it / expensive)

_____

6 We can't take the children to the museum. (it / boring)

_____

7 He can't wear that jacket. (it / small)

_____

3 Complete the second sentence using the words in parentheses and (*not*) *enough* so that it means the same as the first sentence.

1 It's too dirty. (clean)

It *isn't clean enough.*

2 It's too far away. (close)

It _____

3 This town isn't too small for me. (big)

This town _____

4 This book is too boring for me. (interesting)

This book _____

5 I'm too poor to eat here. (rich)

I'm _____

6 I can't lift this heavy box. (strong)

I'm _____

7 It's too noisy to think in here. (quiet)

It _____

8 It's too cold to sunbathe. (hot)

It _____

Present continuous for future plans

4 Complete the sentences using the information.

1 I *'m seeing Bob on* Tuesday.

2 Mr. Sanchez _____ nine thirty.

3 My parents _____ Thursday.

4 I _____ 4 P.M.

5 My sister _____ 10:30.

6 Jack _____ Saturday.

7 We _____ Friday morning.

8 I _____ next week.

5 Write questions about the information in Exercise 4.

1 a) *Who am I seeing on Tuesday?*   Bob.

b) *When am I seeing Bob?*   On Tuesday.

c) *What am I doing on Tuesday?*   I'm seeing Bob.

2 _____

At 9:30.

3 _____

My teacher!

4 _____

Max.

5 _____

She's getting a haircut.

6 _____

On Saturday.

7 _____

On Friday morning.

8 _____

The new Bourne movie.

7

like and *would like*

6 Complete the conversations with the correct form of the verbs in parentheses.

1 **Waiter:** What would you like for dinner, sir?

   Man: I *'d like* (like) the steak, please.

2 **Dad:** Oliver! Wake up! You have homework to do.

   Oliver: Oh, Dad! I _____ (not like) doing homework!

3 **Jackie:** Hey, Rob! Great news! My mom would like _____ (take) us to an Italian restaurant for lunch.

   Rob: Wow, great!

4 **Chris:** Let's take these burgers back to your house.

   Tom: No. My mom _____ (not like) people eating fast food at home. She doesn't like the smell.

5 **Max:** Er, Kate. _____ you _____ (like) to go to the mall tonight?

   Kate: Oh, yes!

6 **Dan:** What kind of music _____ your sister _____ (like) listening to?

   Adam: She likes listening to slow, sad music.

7 Write complete sentences to answer the questions using the information in parentheses.

1 Where would you like to live? (Rio de Janeiro)
   I'd like to live in Rio de Janeiro.

2 What would you like to study? (Portuguese)
   _____

3 What subjects do you like at school? (Spanish and Math)
   _____

4 Who would your sister like to meet? (Taylor Lautner)
   _____

5 Who does your sister like meeting on Saturdays? (her friends)
   _____

6 What car would your dad like to have? (a Ferrari)
   _____

7 What does your mom like doing in her free time? (gardening)
   _____

8 What would your mom like to do tonight? (eat out)
   _____

9 Where does your brother like going on Saturdays? (to concerts)
   _____

10 Where would your brother like to work? (a bank)
   _____

Consolidation

8 Complete the conversation with the correct form of the words in parentheses.

Ben: **1** I *'m doing* (do) something cool tonight.

Andy: What? Come on! Tell me!

Ben: OK. **2** I _____ (meet) Anna.

Andy: Really! Where **3** _____ (you / take) her?

Ben: I don't know. I'd like **4** _____ (take) her to a Mexican restaurant.

Andy: Oh, yeah! There's that new one on King Street.

Ben: No, it **5** _____ (be too expensive) for me. I'm **6** _____ (rich enough) for that! She **7** _____ (like) fast food. I could take her to Jerry's Burgers.

Andy: No, no. It's **8** _____ (cool enough) for a date.

Ben: It **9** _____ (be cool enough) for me!

Andy: OK. It's your date. Good luck!

Indefinite pronoun *one/ones*

That's my **car**.
Which **one**?
The green **one**.

Those are Ben's **shoes**.
Which **ones**?
The big, black **ones**.

Conditional: *if* clause + present

If I watch too much TV, I get a headache.
If she feels hungry, she eats fruit.
If I don't work hard, my mom worries about me.
If I work hard, my mom doesn't worry about me.

What do you do if you are tired?
Where does your sister go if she feels sad?

be like and *look like*

Questions	Answers
What **do** they **look like**?	They are tall and good looking.
What **does** she **look like**?	She is slim with long, dark hair.
What **are** you **like**?	I'm easy-going and friendly.
What **is** he **like**?	He's quiet and shy.
What **is** your school **like**?	It's great.

Adverbs: *a little, kind of, pretty, very, really* + adjective

She's **a little scary**.	They're **pretty nice**.
He's **really tall**.	It's **very quiet** here.
They're **kind of** heavy.	

Notes

Indefinite pronoun *one/ones*

- Use indefinite pronouns to avoid repeating a noun.
- Use *one* for singular count nouns and *ones* for plural nouns.

Conditional: *if* clause + present

Usage

- Use *if* clause + present to say what the result of a true situation is.

Form

- To form an *if* clause + simple present sentence, use: *If* + simple present (action or situation) + comma + simple present (the result).
- The *if* clause can come at the beginning or the end of the sentence. When it comes at the beginning, we put a comma after it.

be like and *look like*

- To answer the question *What is (someone/something) like?*, we usually talk about their personality/qualities.
- To answer the question *What does (someone/something) look like?*, we usually talk about *their/its* appearance.
- We don't use *like* or *look like* in the replies.

Common mistakes

What's Cathy like?
~~*She's like friendly.*~~ ✗
She's friendly. ✓
What does Charles look like?
~~*He looks like tall and handsome.*~~ ✗
He is tall and handsome. ✓

Adverbs: *pretty, a little, kind of, very, really* + adjective

- Use these adverbs before an adjective to say how strong it is. Use *a little, kind of,* and *pretty* to make the adjective weaker. *Really* and *very* make the adjective stronger.
- Use the adverb before the adjective it modifies.

Grammar Practice

Indefinite pronoun *one/ones*

1 **Circle the correct words.**

1 A: Put the glasses on the table.

B: Which *one* / *ones?*

A: The tall *one* / *ones.*

2 A: These flowers are beautiful.

B: The yellow *one* / *ones?*

A: No, the red *one* / *ones* in the garden.

3 A: There's a good soccer game on the other channel.

B: Which *one* / *ones?* We have 250 channels!

4 A: Some of my classmates are taking German classes.

B: Which *one* / *ones?*

A: The *one* / *ones* who like languages.

5 A: Wear your new shirt.

B: Which *one* / *ones?* The blue *one* / *ones?*

A: No, the striped *one* / *ones.*

2 **Read the paragraph. Answer the questions, using *one* or *ones*.**

My house is next to the library. It's a big house. There are three bedroom windows. My bedroom is in the middle. In the yard, you can see some bikes. The two red ones are mine. My dog Benny is in the yard, too. He's very small and very friendly. My parents' car is in the street. It's very old.

1 Which is your house?

It's *the one next to the library* .

2 Is the small house yours?

No, *it isn't*. The *big one is ours*.

3 Which is your bedroom window?

It's _____ .

4 Are the blue bikes yours?

No, _____ . The _____ .

5 Which is your parents' car?

It's _____ .

6 Is the big dog yours?

No, _____ . The _____ .

Conditional: *if* clause + present

3 **Complete the conversations with sentences using *if* clause + present.**

1 A: What do you do if your computer doesn't work?

B: (watch TV)

If my computer *doesn't work, I watch TV.*

2 A: What do you do if your homework is difficult?

B: (ask my sister for help)

If my homework _____

_____ .

3 A: What does your brother do if he has money?

B: (buys video games)

If my brother _____

_____ .

4 A: What does Ana do if she has a problem?

B: (talks to her friends)

If Ana _____

_____ .

5 A: What does your dad do if you come home late?

B: (waits for me in the living room)

If I _____

_____ .

6 A: What does your dog do if you don't give him food?

B: (barks: "Woof woof!")

If I _____

_____ .

4 Write *if* clause + present sentences for each situation and result.

Situation	Result
I get up late	*1 mom – shout at me*
	2 dad – be upset
	3 I – not have breakfast
	4 I – have to run to school

1 If I get up late, <u>my mom shouts at me</u> .

2 If I get up late, _____ .

3 If I get up late, _____ .

4 If I get up late, _____ .

Mom – get home	*5 she – not cook dinner*
late from work	*6 she – not walk the dog*
	7 she – have a long bath

5 If _____ .

6 If _____ .

7 If _____ .

We have a test	*8 I – do lots of work*
at school	*9 Chris – bring five pens!*
	10 Louisa – not worry at all

8 If _____ .

9 If _____ .

10 If _____ .

be like and *look like*

5 Match the questions (1–8) to the answers (a–h).

1 ~~What are you like?~~   *e*

2 What does your brother look like? _____

3 What does your school look like? _____

4 What is your father like? _____

5 What is your sister like? _____

6 What do you look like? _____

7 What is your school like? _____

8 What does your mother look like? _____

a) It's big with lots of windows.

b) She's lazy and bad tempered.

c) I'm short and a little heavy.

d) She's slim and very pretty.

e) I'm quiet and shy.

f) It's great, and the teachers are cool.

g) He's very hard-working and kind of bossy.

h) He's pretty tall and well-built.

6 Write questions and answers using the cues.

1 What / Beyoncé / ?
(very confident)

What's Beyoncé like?

She's very confident.

2 What / Zack Efron / ?
(medium-height with dark brown hair)

What does Zack Efron look like?

He's medium-height with dark brown hair.

3 What / Taylor Swift / ?
(tall with blond hair and big eyes)

_____

_____

4 What / Natalie Portman / ?
(very smart and hard-working)

_____

_____

5 What / Robert Pattinson / ?
(shy and not very confident)

_____

_____

6 What / Joe Jonas / ?
(handsome and not very tall)

_____

_____

Adverbs: *pretty, a little, kind of, very, really* + adjective

7 Rewrite the sentences with the adverb in parentheses in the correct place.

1 This band is good. (pretty)

   This band is pretty good.

2 The clothes they wear are awful. (really)

   _____

3 Mr. Leung is angry today. (very)

   _____

4 His face is red. (really)

   _____

5 I'm tired today because I didn't sleep much. (a little)

   _____

6 He has a bad cough. (really)

   _____

7 Your eyes are red. What's wrong? (very)

   _____

8 That's my sister, but this photo is old and she doesn't have long hair now. (kind of)

   _____

   _____

   _____

8 Write the words in the correct order.

1 is / good / Mr. Gregson / teacher / very / a

   Mr. Gregson is a very good teacher.

2 Darren / sick / now / pretty / is / right

   _____

3 vacation / Costa Rica / Our / great / in / really / was

   _____

4 am / always / on / tired / Fridays / I / really

   _____

5 new / The / students / are / unfriendly / little / a

   _____

6 Inez / unfriendly / today / kind of / is

   _____

7 really / new / This / is / song / great

   _____

8 something / very / Mark / about / upset / is

   _____

Consolidation

9 Complete the blog with words from the box.

> • baggy • little • do • If • is • like • one
> • ones • kind of • wear

What do you wear to parties?

Here are a few of your comments.

Gabby: 1 *If* I go to a party at a friend's house, I always 2 _____ old jeans.

Helen: I have two party dresses. If my red dress is dirty, I wear the blue 3 _____ .

Olga: If I feel 4 _____ relaxed, I wear my old, 5 _____ jeans. If the party 6 _____ special, I wear my new 7 _____ .

Diane: I never know what to wear. I ask everyone the same questions: "What 8 _____ I look 9 _____ in this skirt?" "Is this dress OK?" I always listen to my sister. She's a 10 _____ annoying, but she knows a lot about clothes.

9 Grammar Summary

The definite article with places

the U.S.
the Mediterranean Sea
the Amazon River
the Rocky Mountains

the Atlantic Ocean
the Hawaiian Islands
the Sahara Desert

Present perfect

Affirmative

I've / You've / We've / They've seen this movie.
He's / She's / It's (has) gone out.

Negative

I / You / We / They haven't seen this movie.
He / She / It hasn't gone out.

Questions

Have you arrived?
Has he been here before?

Short answers

Yes, I have. / No, I haven't.
Yes, he has. / No, he hasn't.

Present perfect with *ever* and *never*

Have you ever been to Mexico?
I've never failed a class.

Present perfect with *already* and *yet*

She's already told you the answer.
They haven't contacted us yet.
Have you found your glasses yet?

Simple past and present perfect

I've seen this movie.
I saw this movie two days ago / yesterday / when I was at school.

I've never eaten Mexican food before.
I didn't eat Mexican food last night / on Saturday.

Have you ever been to Russia?
Did you go to Russia last summer / last year / yesterday?

Notes

The definite article with places

- Use the definite article to talk about plural countries and mountains and rivers, seas, oceans, groups of islands, and deserts.

Present perfect

- To form the present perfect, use *have* or *has* + past participle.
- Many irregular verbs have a different past form and past participle. Go to www.pearsonlongman.com/insyc for a list of irregular verbs and their past participles.

Common mistakes

He's went home. ✗
He's gone home. ✓

Present perfect with *ever* and *never*

- Use the present perfect with *ever* and *never* to talk about experiences in your life up to now.
- Use *never* with negative present perfect statements.
- Use *ever* with present perfect questions.

Present perfect with *already* and *yet*

- Use the present perfect with *already* to emphasize that something has happened before now.
- Use the present perfect with *yet* in questions and negative statements to mean *up to now*.

Simple past and present perfect

- Use the simple past with a past time-expression to talk about something that started and finished in the past.
- Use the present perfect to talk about something that started at an unspecified time in the past and has a connection with the present.

Grammar Practice

The definite article with places

1 Circle the correct choices.

1 (The) / – Himalayas are mountains near *the* / (–) India in *the* / (–) Asia.

2 *The* / – Channel Islands are nearer to *the* / – France than to *the* / – U.K.

3 I went to *the* / – New York in *the* / – U.S. last year.

4 *The* / – Nile River goes from *the* / – Africa to *the* / – Mediterranean Sea.

5 *The* / – Atacama Desert in *the* / – South America is drier than *the* / – Sahara Desert.

6 *The* / – West Indies are in *the* / – Caribbean Sea, but *the* / – Hawaiian Islands are in *the* / – Pacific Ocean.

Present perfect

2 Complete the verbs in the chart.

Verb	Past form	Past participle
1 be	w a s / w e r e	b e e n
2 do	d _ _	d _ _ e
3 see	_ a w	s _ e _
4 write	w _ o _ _	w _ _ t _ e _
5 ride	r _ _ e	r _ d _ e _
6 swim	s _ _ m	s _ _ m
7 eat	a _ _	e _ t _ _
8 give	g _ v _	g _ v _ _
9 go	_ e _ _	_ o _ e

3 Complete the sentences. Use the present perfect.

1 Mr. Tomkins *has written* (write) four books.

2 I _____ (make) a movie about my school.

3 Sam _____ (ride) on an elephant and a camel.

4 Our teacher _____ (do) lots of exciting things.

5 Where's my bag? It _____ (go)!

6 Ed _____ (see) this movie. He says it's good.

7 José _____ (eat) fast food in 30 countries!

8 My dad _____ (swim) in four oceans.

Present perfect with *ever* and *never*

4 Write the words in correct sentence order.

1 pizza / never / My / 's / brother / eaten
   My brother's never eaten pizza.

2 I've / been / concert / never / to / a

   _____

3 's / written / never / My / e-mail / an / aunt

   _____

4 horse / Mike / ridden / a / never / 's

   _____

5 I've / in / the / swum / never / sea

   _____

6 never / parents / game / video / have / My / played / a

   _____

   _____

5 Complete the conversation with words from the box.

• been • ever • has • have • haven't
• never • yes

Pablo: 1 *Have* you ever been to Costa Rica?

Marie: No, I 2 _____ . Have you been there?

Pablo: 3 _____ , I have. I've 4 _____ to the jungle there. It's great. The animals are really beautiful.

Marie: Cool. Have you 5 _____ seen a toucan? You know, those birds with colorful beaks?

Pablo: No, I've 6 _____ seen a toucan. But I have seen a tree frog! And my brother 7 _____ even touched one!

6 Write questions and short answers.

1 your friends ever laugh at your hair? (✓)

Have your friends ever laughed at your hair?
Yes, they have.

2 you ever go on a school trip? (✗)

_____

_____

3 your brother ever lose his phone? (✗)

_____

_____

4 your mother ever shout at you? (✓)

_____

_____

5 your father ever do the dishes? (✓)

_____

_____

6 your sister ever come home late? (✗)

_____

_____

Present perfect with *already* and *yet*

7 Look at the list and write sentences with *already* and *yet*.

Before I go on vacation . . .
1 text my friends ✓   5 go to the doctor's ✗
2 get money ✗   6 borrow a laptop ✓
3 buy a train ticket ✗ 7 clean my room ✗
4 wash my clothes ✓   8 pack my clothes ✓

1 _I've already texted my friends._

2 _I haven't gotten money yet._

3 _____

4 _____

5 _____

6 _____

7 _____

8 _____

8 Complete the second sentence using the words in parentheses so that it has a similar meaning to the first sentence. Use the present perfect and *yet* or *already*.

1 I saw this movie a few months ago. (already)

I _'ve already seen this_ movie.

2 I'm going to do my homework later. (done)

I _____ yet.

3 I wrote an e-mail to David last night. (written)

I _____ David.

4 Dad came home a while ago. (come)

Dad _____ home.

5 The test only started ten minutes ago, and I'm doing Question 3. (already)

The test only started ten minutes ago, and I

_____ Question 3.

Simple past and present perfect

9 Circle the correct verb forms.

1 I (wrote) / have written three messages yesterday.

2 We *finished* / *have finished* dinner five minutes ago.

3 I *bought* / *have bought* my first video game when I was ten.

4 I *never failed* / *have never failed* a test.

5 My sister *sang* / *has sung* in concerts, but she *never played* / *has never played* the guitar.

6 *I've already ran* / *I've already run* two miles today!

7 *Did Julie use* / *Has Julie used* her new phone yet?

8 *Did you ever go* / *Have you ever been* to a rock concert?

10 Complete the sentences with the correct form of the verbs provided.

1 **write**

I *'ve written* hundreds of text messages in my life. I *wrote* ten last night.

2 **do**

I _____ my homework when I came home, but I (not) _____ the dishes yet.

3 **have**

We _____ Chinese food last week, but we (never) _____ Japanese food.

4 **make**

My brother _____ two CDs. He _____ the first one two years ago.

5 **give**

My parents _____ me lots of nice presents. Last year, they _____ me a laptop.

6 **go**

My friend _____ to lots of countries. Last summer, she _____ to Brazil.

7 **win**

" _____ you _____ the tennis match yesterday?"

"No. I (never) _____ a match against Jake."

8 **call**

_____ you _____ Rafael last weekend?

_____ you ever _____ him?

11 Rewrite the sentence with a word from the box so that it has the same meaning.

> • a month ago • a week ago • last night
> • last week • three days ago • yesterday

Today is Saturday, June 12.

1 I went to a concert one day ago.

I went to a concert yesterday.

2 My parents went on vacation on June 5.

_____

3 Joe graduated on May 12.

_____

4 I passed the English test on June 9!

_____

5 We watched a good DVD on Friday night, June 11.

_____

6 Ellie and Max were at the beach from June 5 until June 11.

_____

Consolidation

12 Complete the conversation.

Principal: Today, we welcome one of our old students. He's Gary Jones, the famous rock guitarist. Gary is here to answer your questions. Who wants to start?

Student 1: Have you **1** e*ver* played with anyone famous?

Gary: Yes, I **2** h_____ . I've **3** p_____ with Bob Dylan a few times.

Student 1: Who?

Gary: Don't you know Bob Dylan?

Student 1: No. I've **4** n_____ heard of him.

Gary: He's a big star. He **5** w_____ famous in the 1960s.

Student 1: That's a long time ago. My mom was born in 1960!

Student 2: Have you seen the Rolling Stones?

Gary: Of course. I **6** s_____ them last year.

Student 3: Have you **7** b_____ to Bono's house?

Gary: No, I **8** h_____ . I've never met Bono.

Student 4: When **9** d_____ you make your first record?

Gary: I **10** m_____ my first record in 1971.

Student 5: How many songs have you **11** w_____ ?

Gary: About 50.

Student 5: Did you **12** w_____ *Stairway to Heaven*?

Gary: No, I didn't. That was Led Zeppelin. My band was called Dark Clouds.

Students 5: Can you sing us a song?

Gary: Of course. This one's called *My Old School*. I wrote it about this place.

Grammar Summary

will for predictions

Affirmative

I'll (will) be a teacher in the future.

You'll (will) be famous.
He'll (will) have five children.
She'll (will) work on TV.
It'll (will) rain next week.
We'll (will) go to the U.S.
They'll (will) get married.

Negative

I won't be a teacher in the future.
You won't be famous.
He won't have five children.
She won't work on TV.
It won't rain next week.
We won't go to the U.S.
They won't get married.

Questions

Will I meet you again?
Will you pass your exams?
Will he get married?
Will she have children?
Will it rain next week?
Will we work together?
Will they build a house here?

Short answers

Yes, you will. / No, you won't.
Yes, I will. / No, I won't.
Yes, he will. / No, he won't.
Yes, she will. / No, she won't.
Yes, it will. / No, it won't.
Yes, we will. / No, we won't.
Yes, they will. / No, they won't.

Conditional: *if* clause + future

If I go to the mall tonight, I'll see my friends.
If he gets an A, his parents will give him a computer.
If we don't see you tomorrow, we'll call you.
If I don't have any money, I won't buy anything.
If it rains tomorrow, we won't go out.

If Mark doesn't remember your birthday, will you be unhappy?
If Mark doesn't remember your birthday, what will you say?

will for decisions/promises

A: This computer is very old.
B: I'll buy a new one next month. / I won't use it again.

A: You're putting on weight.
B: I know. I'll do more exercise. / I won't eat so much in the future.

will for offers

A: There's a spider in the bathtub.
B: I'll take it out if you want.

Notes

will for predictions

Usage
- Use *will* to talk about things we think or believe will happen in the future.

Form
- For affirmative sentences, use:
  will ('ll) + base form of main verb
- For negative sentences, use:
  won't (*will not*) + base form of main verb
- To form questions, use this word order:
  will + subject
- In short answers, do not repeat the main verb.

Conditional: *if* clause + future

Usage
- Use *if* clause + future to talk about something that may happen in the future, as a result of something else. This structure describes real situations that are likely to happen.

Form
- Use *if* + simple present for the possible future event and *will* + base form of main verb for the result. The two clauses are separated by a comma.
- The two clauses can be written in reverse order without a comma.

Common mistakes
~~If I will work hard, I'll pass my exams.~~ ✗
If I work hard, I'll pass my exams. ✓
~~If we won't hurry, we'll miss the movie.~~ ✗
If we don't hurry, we'll miss the movie. ✓
~~What you will do if you can't find your phone?~~ ✗
What will you do if you can't find your phone? ✓

will for decisions/promises
- Use *will* to talk about decisions or promises to do something.

will for offers
- Use *'ll* (*will*) in statements to offer to do something.

will for predictions

1 Complete the sentences with the correct form of the verbs from the box.

> • be • build • do • drive • grow • listen • ~~live~~
> • speak • use • wear

In the year 2040 . . .

1 people *will live* on Mars.

2 we _____ flying cars.

3 people _____ computers in their clothes.

4 robots _____ all our housework.

5 families _____ food in their homes.

6 the world _____ a clean and happy place.

7 we _____ every language in the world using special computers.

8 people _____ houses under the sea.

9 young people _____ to strange music.

10 we _____ less oil.

2 Correct the sentences using the words in parentheses.

1 A: In 20 years, I'll have a big house. (✗ palace)

  B: *No, you won't. You'll have a palace!*

2 A: In ten years, you'll be my assistant. (✗ boss)

  B: _____

    _____

3 A: In five years, I'll be a poor artist. (✗ rich)

  B: _____

4 A: Jake will pass all his exams this year. (✗ most of)

  B: _____

    _____

5 A: Chris will move to Brazil one day. (✗ Chile)

  B: _____

6 A: In 50 years, this school will have 2,000 students. (✗ everyone will study at home)

  B: _____

    _____

3 Look at the predictions and complete the questions.

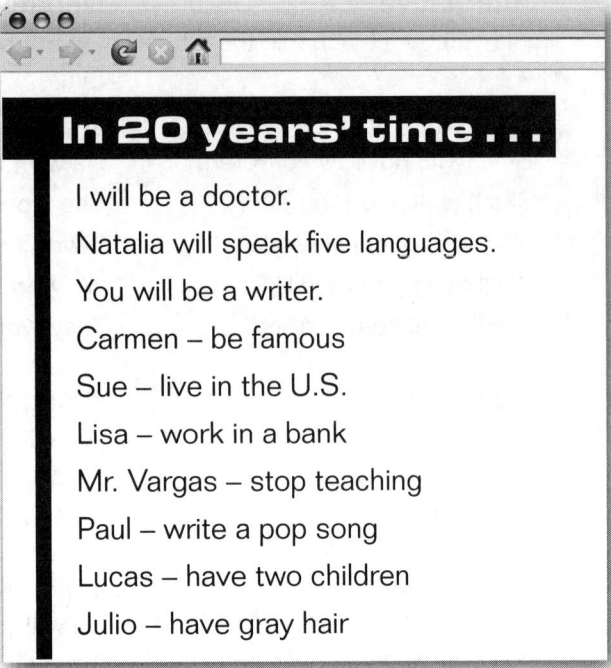

In 20 years' time . . .

I will be a doctor.

Natalia will speak five languages.

You will be a writer.

Carmen – be famous

Sue – live in the U.S.

Lisa – work in a bank

Mr. Vargas – stop teaching

Paul – write a pop song

Lucas – have two children

Julio – have gray hair

1 A: Who *will be a* doctor?

  B: I will.

2 A: What _____ be?

  B: A writer.

3 A: Where _____ ?

  B: In the U.S.

4 A: _____ a teacher?

  B: No, he won't.

5 A: How many _____ ?

  B: Two.

6 A: Who _____ languages?

  B: Natalia.

7 A: _____ famous?

  B: Yes, she will.

8 A: Where _____ ?

  B: In a bank.

9 A: What _____ ?

  B: A pop song.

10 A: _____ gray hair?

  B: Yes, he will.

Conditional: *if* clause + future

4 Match the beginnings of the sentences (1–8) to the endings (a–h).

1 ~~If you don't work hard,~~ _c_

2 If you open that e-mail, _____

3 What will you wear _____

4 If the bus is late, _____

5 Who will Rafael play next _____

6 Will your sister study French _____

7 If you're hungry later, _____

8 If I see Esteban later, _____

> a) I'll walk to school.
>
> b) I'll make you a pizza.
>
> c) you'll fail your classes.
>
> d) if she goes to college?
>
> e) I'll tell him about the concert.
>
> f) you'll get a virus.
>
> g) if he wins this game?
>
> h) if your skirt is dirty?

5 Complete the second sentence so that it means the same as the first.

1 If you go to bed now, you won't be tired tomorrow.

If you don't go to bed now, _you'll be tired tomorrow_.

2 If Wayne doesn't play, we'll lose.

If Wayne plays, _____ .

3 If I see Tom, I'll borrow his bike.

_____ , I won't borrow his bike.

4 If my dad gets time off, we'll go camping.

_____ , we won't go camping.

5 If my mom drives us to the party, we'll be early.

If my mom doesn't drive us to the party,

_____ .

6 If the party is boring, I'll go home at 10 P.M.

If the party isn't boring, _____

_____ .

will for decisions/promises

6 Write the verb in parentheses in the correct form using *will* or *won't*.

1 My computer is very old. (buy)

I'll buy a new one.

2 These cups are dirty. (not / use)

OK. _I won't use_ them.

3 We're hungry. (cook)

_____ some dinner.

4 I'm too tired to clean my room now. (do)

_____ it later.

5 My mom's tired. (make)

_____ her a cup of coffee.

6 There's some good free software on this website. (download)

_____ it.

7 I didn't do very well in my classes. (not / be)

_____ so lazy next year.

8 My dad's asleep. (not / play)

_____ loud music because we don't want to wake him up.

will for offers

7 Write the words in sentence order to complete the conversations.

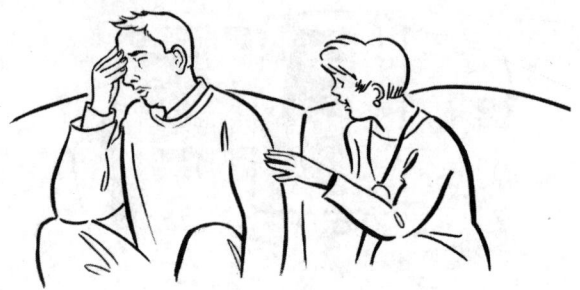

A Mr. Garcia: I don't feel well.

Mrs. Garcia: **1** call / the / I'll / doctor

I'll call the doctor.

Mr. Garcia: No, it's OK. I'll go to bed.

Mrs. Garcia: **2** get / I'll / a / of / you / glass / water.

_____

B Cameron: I'm bored. I have nothing to do.

Sean: **3** DVD / I'll / a / you / lend / you / if / want.

_____

Cameron: No, my DVD player's broken.

Sean: OK. **4** I'll / one / games. / my / get / of / video

_____

Cameron: OK. That sounds good.

C Louisa: **5** for / something / I'll / dinner. / cook

_____

Jamie: No, it's OK. You have lots of work to do.

Louisa: **6** a / you / pizza / I'll / like. / order / if

_____

Jamie: Yum. Cheese and mushroom for me!

D Dad: This computer is really slow.

Son: **7** I'll / at / look / it.

_____

Dad: Thanks, but I need a new one.

Son: **8** I'll / choose / if / help / you / you / want. / one

_____

Dad: OK, but nothing too expensive.

Consolidation

8 Circle the correct answers and write the words.

Hi Ramón,

Do you ever think about the future? In three years, we'll graduate. It's not long!
1 *Will we* do well in our classes? What will we do if we **2** _____ pass them? What
3 _____ our teachers say? What will our parents say? I know what you're thinking. If
we **4** _____ hard, we **5** _____ OK. And you're right, but you know I like to worry!
I started thinking about the future because I read a website about taking time off before
college. It was great. I think if I get into college, **6** _____ a year off to travel and
work before I start classes. **7** _____ to Africa or Asia, and **8** _____ amazing
things. I talked about it with my brother. He's going to college next year. He said: "If you
take a year off, **9** _____ ? If you travel, you'll be bored and you **10** _____ any
money." He isn't interested in traveling at all. Oh well, I guess I have three years to think
about it!

See you soon, Lourdes

1 a) We will   b) We'll   c) Will we

2 a) don't   b) won't   c) aren't

3 a) will we   b) will they   c) will

4 a) work   b) will work   c) worked

5 a) are   b) be   c) 'll be

6 a) I'm taking   b) I'll take   c) I take

7 a) I'll go   b) I go   c) If I go

8 a) I'll see   b) I see   c) I'm seeing

9 a) what do you do   b) what will you do

   c) what are you doing

10 a) don't have   b) will have   c) won't have

Grammar Summary

should/shouldn't

Affirmative

I / You / We / They **should work** harder.

He / She **should go** to bed.

It **should be** easy.

Negative

I / You / We / They **shouldn't eat** fast food.

He / She **shouldn't drink** coffee.

It **shouldn't take** long.

Questions

Should I **work** tonight?

Should she **go** there?

Short answers

Yes, you **should**.

No, she **shouldn't**.

have to/don't have to

Affirmative

I / You / We / They **have to get up** at six o'clock.

He / She **has to take** some medicine.

It **has to** arrive soon.

Negative

I / You / We / They **don't have to get up** at six o'clock.

He / She **doesn't have to take** any medicine.

It **doesn't have to** take that long.

Questions

Do you **have to study**?

Does he **have to do** chores?

Short answers

Yes, I **do**. / No, I **don't**.

Yes, he **does**. / No, he **doesn't**.

had to/didn't have to

Affirmative

I / You / He / She / We / They **had to get up** at six o'clock.

It **had to stop** there.

Negative

I / You / He / She / We / They **didn't have to get up** at six o'clock.

It **didn't have to** stop there.

Questions

Did you **have to work** last Sunday?

Short answers

Yes, I **did**. / No, I **didn't**.

Notes

should/shouldn't

Usage

- Use *should* and *shouldn't* + base form of main verb to give and ask for advice.

Form

- For affirmative statements, use: *should* + base form of main verb.
- For negatives, use: *shouldn't* + base form of main verb.
- To form questions, use this word order: *should* + subject.
- In short answers, we do not repeat the main verb.

Common mistake

~~What I should do?~~ ✗

What should I do? ✓

have to/don't have to had to/didn't have to

Usage

- Use *have to* + base form of main verb to say that something is necessary. Use *don't have to* when something is not necessary. Use *had to* to talk about obligations in the past.

Form

- For affirmative statements, use *have* with *I, you, we,* and *they,* and *has* with *he, she,* and *it*. For simple past sentences, use *had to* in all forms.
- For negative statements, use *don't/doesn't* + *have to* in the simple present or *didn't* + *have to* in the simple past.
- Use *do/does* + subject + *have to* for simple present questions and *did* + subject + *have to* for simple past questions.
- For short answers, use *do/don't* or *does/doesn't* in the simple present and *did/didn't* in the simple past.

Common mistakes

~~Have you to get up early?~~ ✗

Do you have to get up early? ✓

~~What time he has to go to bed?~~ ✗

What time does he have to go to bed? ✓

should/shouldn't

1 Look at the advice. Complete the sentences using *should* and *shouldn't*.

Have a healthy lifestyle

Good things to do	Bad things to do
Go to bed early	Drink lots of coffee
Get lots of exercise	Stay up all night
Eat fruit and vegetables	Eat fast food
Drink water	Smoke
Relax	Worry about things

1 *You should go to* _____ bed early.

2 _____ lots of exercise.

3 _____ lots of coffee.

4 _____ all night.

5 _____ fruit and vegetables.

6 _____ water.

7 _____ fast food.

8 _____ smoke.

9 _____ relax.

10 _____ about things.

2 Complete the questions.

Your questions answered

1 What time *should I go* to bed?

There's no correct answer, but try to get eight hours of sleep a night.

2 How much exercise _____ ?

You should get about an hour a day.

3 What food _____ ?

You should eat fruit and vegetables.

4 How much water _____ ?

You should drink about eight glasses of water a day.

5 How _____ ?

You should relax by listening to music or doing anything that helps you forget about homework or problems.

6 _____ medicine to relax?

No, you shouldn't. Only take medicine when your doctor tells you it's OK.

have to/don't have to

3 Look at the chart. Write affirmative sentences using the cues.

	My parents	Me	My brother	My sister	My friends
Do the dishes	✗	✓	✓	✗	✗
Clean room	✓	✓	✓	✓	✗
Make dinner	✓	✗	✗	✓	✗
Do the vacuuming	✓	✗	✓	✗	✓
Do the ironing	✗	✓	✗	✓	✗

1 I / do the dishes   *I have to do the dishes.* _____

2 My sister / make dinner   _____

3 My parents / clean their room   _____

4 My brother / clean his room   _____

5 My parents / make dinner   _____

6 My friends / do the vacuuming   _____

7 My sister / do the ironing   _____

4 Write negative sentences using the information in Exercise 3.

1 My parents / dishes
My parents don't have to do the dishes.

2 I / make dinner

_____

3 My brother / ironing

_____

4 My sister / vacuuming

_____

5 My friends / make dinner

_____

6 I / vacuuming

_____

7 My parents / ironing

_____

8 My sister / dishes

_____

5 Write questions using the cues. Then use the information in Exercise 3 to write answers.

1 your parents / dishes?
Do your parents have to do the dishes?
No, they don't.

2 you / clean your room?

_____

_____

3 your brother / make dinner?

_____

_____

4 your friends / do the ironing

_____

_____

5 your sister / clean her room?

_____

_____

6 you / do the vacuuming?

_____

_____

7 your friends / clean their rooms?

_____

_____

had to/didn't have to

6 Complete the questions and answers.

1 *Did* you *have to do* homework when you were in elementary school? (**✗**)
No, I didn't.

2 _____ your brother _____ wear a uniform when he was in elementary school? (✓)

_____

3 _____ your dad _____ start work at 6 A.M. last year? (✓)

_____

4 _____ you _____ walk to school last week? (✓)

_____

5 _____ Cathy _____ eat school lunches last year? (✗)

_____

6 _____ your parents _____ take tests when they were in elementary school? (✗)

_____

7 _____ your cousin Peter _____ work last summer? (✓)

_____

8 _____ your sister _____ play rugby when she was in school? (✗)

_____

7 Complete the sentences about the two vacations using the correct form of *have to* in the simple past with the verbs in parentheses.

| two years ago | last year |

1 Two years ago, we *didn't have to take* our passports. Last year, we *had to take* our passports. (take)

2 Two years ago, we _____ our vacation because the campsite is usually never full. Last year, we _____ our vacation in January! (book)

3 Two years ago, we _____ our food on a small fire. Last year, we _____ our food. We ate in the hotel restaurant. (cook)

4 Two years ago, we _____ 200 feet to the bathroom in the middle of the night. Last year, we _____ far—we had our own bathroom. (walk)

5 Two years ago, we _____ the dishes. Last year, we _____ the dishes. (do)

6 Two years ago, we _____ a lot of money. Last year, we _____ a lot of money because the hotel was very expensive. (spend)

7 Two years ago, we _____ a tent, chairs, a table, and other things. Last year, we only _____ our clothes. (take)

8 Two years ago, we _____ nice clothes. Last year, we _____ nice clothes every day in the hotel restaurant. (wear)

Consolidation

8 Circle the correct choices.

Hector: This project is hard. We **1** *don't have to / had to /* (should) start now.

Victor: OK. What **2** *should we / we have to / we should* do first?

Hector: We **3** *should / has / have* to find some information about three countries.
We **4** *should / has to / had to* use the computer and these library books.

Victor: OK. How much **5** *do we have / should we / we have* to write?

Hector: We **6** *shouldn't / don't / aren't* have to write too much. About two pages for each country.

Victor: That's easy.

Hector: Really? Do you want to write it all?

Victor: No, no. It's OK. I wrote the last project with Ernesto. He's so lazy. I **7** *have to / has to / had to* write everything.

Hector: Why **8** *did you have / you had / do you have* to work with Ernesto?

Victor: I **9** *hadn't / didn't / don't*. I wanted to. He's my friend. Never again, though.

Hector: You **10** *shouldn't / don't have to / didn't have to* work with friends. It's not a good idea.

Victor: Er, Hector. We're friends.

Hector: Oh, yes. Sorry!

Grammar Summary

Infinitives of purpose

I went to the zoo **to see** the baby animals.
A: Why did you get up so early? B: **To do** my homework.

so + adjective + that

It's **so hot that** I can't sleep.
They're **so worried** about the test **that** they don't want to eat.

would ('d) rather

Affirmative

I**'d rather play** soccer (**than go** swimming).
They**'d rather watch** a movie (**than do** their homework).

Negative

I**'d rather not play** soccer.
They**'d rather not watch** a movie.

Questions

Would you rather go out
   (**than/stay**) at home?
Would he rather sit in the yard?

Short answers

Yes, I **would**. / No, I **wouldn't**.

Yes, he **would**. / No, he **wouldn't**.

would ('d) prefer

Affirmative

We**'d prefer to eat** now (**than to wait** until later).
She**'d prefer to go** home (**than to stay** here).

Negative

We**'d prefer not to eat** now.
She**'d prefer not to go** home.

Questions

Would you prefer to leave?
Would he prefer to wear jeans?

Short answers

Yes, I **would**. / No, I **wouldn't**.
Yes, he **would**. / No, he **wouldn't**.

Notes

Infinitives of purpose

- Use infinitives of purpose to give a reason for doing something.

Common mistake
~~I called Mia for to ask her out.~~ ✗
I called Mia to ask her out. ✓

so + adjective + that

- Use *so* + adjective + *that* to talk about extreme situations that lead to a result.

would ('d) rather; would ('d) prefer

Usage
- Use *would rather* or *would prefer* to say someone would like to do one activity more than another.

Form
- To form negatives, add *not* after the verb *prefer/rather*.
- For questions, use **or** to separate two things and ask which of the things the person would rather do.
- Use *than* with *rather* to state a preference between two options.

Common mistakes
~~I'd rather to go out.~~ ✗
I'd rather go out. ✓
~~She'd prefer cook dinner.~~ ✗
She'd prefer to cook dinner. ✓
~~We'd rather don't go home.~~ ✗
We'd rather not go home. ✓

Infinitives of purpose

1 Complete the sentences with the correct form of the verbs from the box.

> • eat • go • learn • meet • save • ~~see~~

1 We're going to the theater *to see* a movie.

2 We went to the coffee shop _____ our friends.

3 My parents always walk to work _____ on gas.

4 Our cat only comes into the kitchen _____ her dinner.

5 I got up early _____ jogging before school.

6 Our class is going to a museum next week _____ about the history of our town.

2 Combine the sentences using an infinitive of purpose.

1 Jack went to his aunt's house. He wanted to see his cousin.

   Jack went to his aunt's house to see his cousin.

2 My mom came to my school. She had to speak to my teacher.

   _____

   _____

3 We had a day off from school today. We studied for our test.

   _____

   _____

4 We take our dog to the park every day. We need to give him some exercise.

   _____

   _____

5 Angie and José had a party. They were celebrating their 15th birthdays.

   _____

   _____

6 My friends are going to Seattle next week. They're going to see a baseball game.

   _____

   _____

so + adjective + that

3 Complete the sentences using so . . . that and the adjectives from the box.

> • big • excited • ~~expensive~~ • hot
> • late • tired • upset • young

1 My dad's new car was *so expensive that* he's scared to drive it!

2 My mom was _____ she called my dad at work.

3 Manuel was _____ about his birthday _____ he didn't sleep at all.

4 Our English teacher is _____ he looks like a student.

5 We were _____ my parents were already asleep.

6 I was _____ I fell asleep at 9 P.M.

7 Our school is _____ I don't know where all the rooms are.

8 It was _____ I wore shorts.

4 Combine the sentences using *so* + adjective + *that*.

1 Mark was very busy. He didn't come to my party.

Mark was so busy that he didn't come to my party.

2 I was late for school. I had to run all the way.

_____

_____

3 Our car is very small. My dad can't sit in the back.

_____

_____

4 I was bored on my vacation. I wanted to come home.

_____

_____

5 Tracy's sister is very old. She remembers The Beatles.

_____

_____

6 The movie ended late. I missed the last bus home.

_____

_____

would ('d) rather; would ('d) prefer

5 Make and write sentences using *rather* and the information in the table.

	Play basketball or soccer ?	Eat Chinese food or fast food?	Go to France or Italy?
James	basketball	Chinese food	France
Me	soccer	Chinese food	Italy
Molly and Liz	basketball	fast food	France

1 James (basketball / soccer)

James would rather play basketball than soccer.

_____

2 I (France / Italy)

I'd rather go to Italy than to France.

_____

3 I (Chinese food / fast food)

_____

_____

4 Molly and Liz (France / Italy)

_____

_____

5 James (France / Italy)

_____

_____

6 Molly and Liz (basketball / soccer)

_____

_____

7 James (Chinese food / fast food)

_____

_____

8 I (basketball / soccer)

_____

_____

6 Make and write negative sentences using the information in the pictures and in Exercise 6.

1 I'd prefer _not to play basketball_ .

2 Molly and Liz would rather _____

_____ .

3 James would prefer _____

_____ .

4 Molly and Liz would prefer _____

_____ .

5 James would rather _____

_____ .

6 I'd prefer _____

_____ .

7 Write questions using the cues.

1 you / prefer / do homework / have a test?

Would you prefer to do homework or have a test?

2 your dad / rather / drive / travel by train?

_____

_____

3 your friends / rather / watch soccer / play soccer?

_____

_____

4 your mom / prefer / go to a restaurant / go to a concert?

_____

_____

5 you / rather / read a book / listen to music?

_____

_____

6 your dog / prefer / take a walk / sleep?

_____

_____

8 Rewrite the sentences using the verbs in parentheses.

1 I'd rather go shopping. (prefer)
   I'd prefer to go shopping.

2 My sister would prefer to stay at home. (rather)
   My sister would rather stay at home.

3 I'd rather not go out tonight. (prefer)

   _____

4 They would prefer not to have a party. (rather)

   _____

5 Where would you rather go? (prefer)

   _____

6 What would you prefer to eat? (rather)

   _____

7 Would your brother prefer to come with us? (rather)

   _____

8 Would you rather eat somewhere else? (prefer)

   _____

Consolidation

9 Match the beginnings of the sentences (1–9) to the correct endings (a–i).

1 This is so _c_

2 I'd rather not _____

3 Tim went to the post office _____

4 The movie was so boring that _____

5 I'd rather eat now _____

6 Would you rather play tennis _____

7 I'd prefer not _____

8 Our vacation was so much fun _____

9 What would you _____

a) I fell asleep in the theater.

b) prefer to do, go for a walk or stay at home?

c) hard that I can't do it.

d) or go swimming?

e) that we're going there again next year.

f) go to the beach today.

g) than wait until four o'clock.

h) to go shopping today.

i) to mail a present to his friend.